The Circles *God* Draws

A Memoir
by Ruth Holland Scott

ISBN 978-0-9891209-1-3

Published by Herons Bend Productions 2013

heronsbendproductions.com
Ruth Rosenberg-Naparsteck, editor, publisher
Cover design by Morgan Martin
Book design by Megan Sperber, Austin Design3D
Photography by Denise Batiste
Candid family photographs by William Gregory Scott

Table of Contents

This memoir is dedicated to my husband, the love of my life, and my children, grandchildren and great grandchildren who inherit this world.

May the circles that radiate from their lives create goodness in every part of this world.

Acknowledgments

I acknowledge the tremendous encouragement given to me through Divine Grace and the people who loved me enough to encourage me to be my own person: my mother and father, brothers Bob and Bill, my sister June, and Gant and Holland cousins, Donna Jean, Beverly, Vernelis, and more friends than I can name. I thank my editor and publisher, Ruth Rosenberg Naparsteck, for her hours of interviews, reviews, writing guidance and editing as we worked for more than five years writing my memoirs. Without our team effort and growing friendship, this book might never have been written.

I thank Richard Peck, director of Rare Books Division of the University of Rochester, Rush Rhees Library, who collected and organized my official papers and encouraged me by asking, "When are you going to write your book? It's important." I thank Lydia Boddie-Rice for her friendship and encouragement and design assistance on my publicity. To Megan Sperber for her book design and Jen Moritz for her proofreading. To Morgan Martins for her observations, design and publicizing.

To the people I have worked with over the years in banks and corporations, in education and civic, as well as in public service, I extend my heartfelt thanks for enriching my life. Among those people are Connie Mitchell, Gwen Martins, Bill Sullivan, Connie Gross, J. K. Langkans, Marian Johnson, Ruby and Gene Lockhart, Margaret Sanchez, Linda Weinstein, Jennifer Leonard, Shirley Thompson, Gwen Darisaw, Liz Brown and Dr. Walter Cooper.

To Norma Brand, the Wilsons, the Kamells, the Fergusons, the Smiths, the Hendersons, church families at Lewis Chapel A.M.E Zion in Albion, Michigan; Antioch Baptist in Cleveland, Ohio; Delevan United Methodist, Memorial A.M.E. Zion, Trinity United Methodist and Genesee Baptist in Rochester, New York. Thank you for your spiritual nurturing. A special thanks to Betty Strasenburgh, Randy and Marian Henderson, Lois Posner and Deborah Witt.

Introduction

Years ago, when I was on Rochester's City Council, my husband, Bill, and I sat next to author Alex Haley at an intimate dinner. He had recently published his book *Roots*. We talked about the meaning of life and his search for that meaning in the "roots" of his own family. He said that, regardless of personal life circumstances, we find strength in the lives of our ancestors. That point was strong in his blockbuster book and the subsequent movie.

A few years ago, with the birth of our grandchildren and great grandson, I reached the stage in life when I have *become* that ancestor—searching for my own roots and recognizing the "circles God draws" in our lives. I have become that ancestral link between our children and our ancestors—my life extending that circle.

The play *Cry the Beloved Country* contains the repeated musical theme that we are not alone—not lost in the stars—and that God watches over all of us no matter how small a "star" we might be. That little girl on the cover of this book is me at three and a half years of age—just beginning the life adventure that is still unfolding—a little star.

When I was born prematurely, I did not have a developed voice. My parents were afraid that I might cry and they would not hear me, so they took turns holding me in their arms in fear that I might choke or need something. Little did they know that, because of their watchfulness, I grew up with a strong voice that I now share with you—the reader.

My mother, Edna Brown Holland, at about ten years old. I see the calm young lady who had already lost her parents and was living with her aunt in the loving care of her extended family. She seemed confident for the challenging life ahead of her. It was that confidence that she passed on to her children.

The Inheritance of
Our Mother's Shackles and Power
—*Ruth Holland Scott*

The shackles in our lives
Are the combining chemistry between
Our Mother's obligations to
Hold life together with safety pins and scotch tape,
Knotted ropes and sealed boxes and
Their persistence. Their existence
Was in living tight rope consistencies,
"An outside the body experience,"
That held at bay the pain of rejection
The suffocation of spirit, mystically bound
Between heaven and earth by prescribed roles;
Slave ... girl ... daughter ... mother ... other,

Something ... Miss Thing ... Noth-i-n-g!
Teachers, preachers, politicians and pimps
Crushed them between their ideologies, theologies,
Politicizing and "mis-usings."

The power in our lives
Is the divine spirit of freedom's
Fulfilling of itself.
That power courses through our voices in song.
With busy hands, undulating spirits
And rhythmic dance.

We are in defiance of all captivity
Because we know the secret of our muse.
A wellspring of joy bubbles up through troubled worlds and
Troubled times.
We were fashioned by a creator who makes butterfly wings.
And that is why the Mona Lisa smiles
And this the connection between
"Caged Birds" and "Phenomenal women!"

Leila Hegwood, mother's first cousin, who was raised as a sister by Aunt Corrie (Nannie) and Uncle Henry. Mother used to lament that when she and Leila wore identical dresses, Mother always looked better. Leila was my godmother. She never recovered from the loss of her infant daughter.

My Inheritance

Although we each must seek and find life's purpose, much of who we are—body and soul—is inherited from our ancestors more closely our parents and grandparents. When I look back on my life, I can remember what my dad and mother modeled for us as children. What they did in their everyday lives served us in our own lives as we children became parents ourselves.

My mother's parents were from Pensacola, Florida, and my dad's from Waycross, Georgia. Both of my parents were orphaned as young children—my mother around the age of seven; my father, about six. They were both informally taken in by relatives, as was the tradition then. Court records give clues to these informal "adoptions." About 1912, my mother, along with another child, Lelia Hegwood, is registered as living with her Aunt Corrie and Uncle Henry Taylor.

My mother's memory of her youth was fragmentary. She did not remember her mother, Derby Gantt, or much about her father, Joseph Brown. I think they lived along a river where her father worked as a fisherman. While my mother did not remember her mother, she did recall "Grandma Autry," who spoke French and wore her long black hair in tresses, suggesting a Black Foot Indian heritage. Mom had two brothers, Joe and Bill. I never met Joe and we never knew what happened to him. Mom had a photograph of him—a male version of herself—light skinned, penetrating eyes and an engaging smile. Bill, on the other hand, had skin of dark chocolate brown and light-colored eyes. On Uncle Bill's only visit to Albion, I remember his hearty laugh and the red and blue plaid dress with silk-lined pockets and sleeves, which he let me pick out at the children's dress shop in downtown Albion.

About the time my mother was taken in by the Taylors, the family moved to Albion, Michigan, with the great migration of other men of color attracted to work in the factories and foundries. Hungry for manpower between 1910 and 1920, growing companies sent recruiters, enticing *men* of color (not their families) to work in the North and providing one-way bus tickets. Uncle Henry turned down the one-way tickets and, with his wife and adopted daughters (Lelia Gardner and Edna Brown—cousins to each other and daughters of two Gantt sisters), took the train to Albion, Michigan. Uncle Henry and Aunt Corrie (Nannie) never lived in the

Four of the five Gant men with their father, Uncle Buddy, in the front yard of their house. Uncle Buddy, my mother's first cousin from Pensacola, Florida, kept a garden that helped feed the large family. A "Jack of All Trades," he also worked at Gail Manufacturing Company and engaged my father in selling shoes, clothing and insurance on the side.

Uncle Buddy with his four daughters—all Gant cousins—and an unidentified woman. The brothers and girls supported the Holland family and attended special award ceremonies and events to support me—from my directing of a school junior play to my award of an honorary doctorate from Albion College in Michigan.

small, poorly constructed company housing. I think maybe they gathered a nest egg while Uncle Henry worked on the loading docks in Pensacola. They either rented or owned a house nestled between a bridge crossing the Kalamazoo River and gas tanks and a coal yard across from the railroad station in Albion.

I am not certain what job Uncle Henry took, but I believe he was a foreman for the Gail Manufacturing Company in Albion.

Dad saw his mother for the last time when he was about six or seven years old. His Aunt Maggie Crooms was speaking harshly to his mother and she was in tears. He and his brother, William, were moved to Detroit, Michigan, and were taken in to stay with the Reverend Crooms family, wearing the hand-me-down clothes of their nine boys, having little to eat, and remembering harsh treatment and no affection. There was a lock on the telephone and the refrigerator. The "spare the rod and spoil the child" mentality of the Crooms' household also held that once a male child turned twelve, he should leave school and go to work to help support the nine boys and one girl in the family. Dad and his brother made twelve.

Dad did not adapt to city life. He and his brother were born in the rural town of Waycross, Georgia. So, in the summer, Dad used to walk the streets of Detroit and was sometimes picked up by the Salvation Army bus that drove the streets looking for idle kids to take to summer day camp. Dad recalled that he got a full meal, and occasionally socks and gloves. He learned songs and poetry that he passed on to us kids. He memorized every poem in *Beloved Poems of the American People*.

I asked Dad what he did to keep himself from being afraid as he walked the streets of the sprawling city. He told me he whistled. Try as I might to position my mouth, my tongue and my teeth, no whistle passed my lips. So at the age of ten, when walking home from church in the dark, having left off my friends at various turning points, I sang hymns at the top of my voice. By the age of eleven, the fear dissipated.

While walking the streets, Dad often dropped into the train station, where he would listen to the stops as they were called over the loud speaker. He dreamed about traveling to these far-away places. He liked the sound of Albion.

Dad said he never would have quit school if it hadn't been for a man-to-man conversation his uncle had with him, announcing that he thought

Dad was old enough to go to work and share the burden of supporting the family. Next, Dad had a spirit-crushing experience in Detroit job hunting when he was enticed by billboards to apply to Ford Motor Company. Billboards called, "Ford Wants You" and "Come and Start Your Career—Up the Ladder With Ford."

So one day, Dad walked miles from home in his best raggedy clothes, newspaper filling the holes in his shoes, hands in his pockets and whistling all the way to the front door of the Ford office. The security guard met him at the door and demanded to know where Dad intended to go. Dad proudly announced, "I'm here to secure my future at the Ford Motor Company."

The guard responded, "You snotty-nosed (expletive deleted) nigger. You better get out of my sight before I have you arrested."

Given that job-hunting experience, Dad hopped a train to Albion, where he applied to Malleable Iron Works and became a machinist. Even running away did not stop the uncle who learned where he was working and claimed ownership of Dad's pay. Dad had to go to the office to require that they pay him only and to return his pay to him. The company agreed and later told his uncle that Dad had left their employ and left no forwarding address.

On Ann Street, I still remember pushing my baby brother, Gilbert, in his stroller up to the very busy Austin Avenue intersection, less than a block from my house, as I told him that he must never try to cross this street by himself. Needless to say, my mother was not at all happy to find me taking this initiative with my baby brother. Gilbert died from a hole in his heart soon after, when I was only three or four years old. His passing was difficult for me to grasp as a child. I thought God might have been punishing me because I had disobeyed my parents by leaving the front of our house pushing his stroller; but my mother assured me that Gilbert died from the hole in his heart. It was God's will. He now lived in Heaven with God.

My mother helped me realize that death was a part of life and not to be feared or to be angry about. As I sat in the pew in front of the window of the "old" Lewis Chapel A.M.E. Church, I used to hold conversations with Gilbert, telling him God would take care of him. I promised I would be good so that I could someday join him.

Gilbert with Dad. Gilbert's death as an infant left a big hole in my heart. I am saddened that my siblings did not know him.

My sister and me at a young age. I first heard of my sister's birth from the choir director at church, who met me on the street and said, "You have a beautiful new baby sister and you will no longer be the apple of your parents' eyes. And besides, she is prettier than you."
I, of course, denied it because I had no idea my mother was in the hospital to have a baby. Although it took me a few weeks, I adopted my sister as my own baby doll. We grew over the years to be friends and confidantes.

For a reason that I have never fully understood, when I was five and a half years old, we left our tree-lined neighborhood on Ann Street to live with Uncle Henry and Aunt Corrie, whom we called Nannie. I think maybe we moved because she couldn't pay the rent alone or because Mom wanted to save money for a house and Dad was in the tuberculosis sanitarium. She was also expecting her fourth child (counting Gilbert), my brother Bob. When I look back on Mom and Dad, they seemed to take so much in stride.

Nannie had a debilitating stroke when she was only twenty-seven years old. It left her lame on one side and unable, I think, to have children of her own. She was a tall, heavy-set woman with a pecan complexion who walked somewhat gracefully with a cane. She seemed very stern to me; but my sister June seemed to love Nannie more than she loved anyone else in the family. Whenever June was in trouble at home, she could be found at Nannie's house.

Our two-story Eaton Street home always seemed smaller to me than the single-story Ann Street house we first lived in; perhaps because I was smaller and the family consisted only of Mother and Father and Gilbert and I. Before we moved to Eaton Street, June, was born. That house was so small that she jumped off of the couch set against one wall and landed on her knees on the heat register against the other wall. I would guess the room was about six by seven. June used to get into trouble because I would dare her to do things that we were forbidden to do and she stubbornly did whatever *she* was forbidden to do. She still has the scars from the register burn. The coal-fired furnace was in the earthen basement opposite the washing machine and rinse tub. Before that furnace was installed, we had a pot-bellied stove in the center of the living room. We used it to cook, boil water and heat the living room.

In Nannie's house, my sister, brother and I stayed in one tiny bedroom on the second floor. Mom and Dad, when he wasn't in the tuberculosis sanitarium, stayed in the second bedroom at the top of the stairs. The first floor was divided into three small areas: a living room, kitchen with a small counter and ice box, and a small bedroom.

My mother used to say our bedtime prayers with us:
Now I lay me down to sleep;
I pray the Lord my soul to keep.
If I should die before I wake

I pray the Lord my soul to take.

Then we recited the *Lord's Prayer* and listed all those whom we wanted God to bless, starting with each other and Mom and Dad. When the list seemed unending, Mom said, "Amen."

The hallway between my parents' and our bedroom was not much wider than the steps. My brother Bob was born at Nannie's home in Mom and Dad's bedroom. He soon took his place in a bassinet in the corner of their room. I remember awakening one morning to the cry of a baby. Knocking on the door of my parents' bedroom where this new sound was coming from, I opened it to hear a baby yelling at the top of his lungs.

Mom said, "Meet your new brother, Robert, Jr."

I said, "How did you know I wanted a baby brother?"

Such a wonder it was to me. I never noticed my mother was having a baby. In those days, pregnancies were not discussed; particularly with children.

As I grew older, I realized my mother needed help because she was working three jobs: cleaning the Bohm Theatre, waiting tables and cooking at Albion College, and preparing a white family's children for school every day. I thought I would wash the laundry. I knew Mother would be tired when she came home from work. My brother Bill was born by then, and she used to take him with her and tie him to a seat in the Bohm Theatre while she cleaned. After Nannie went to bed and the snores confirmed her sleep, I sneaked down the stairs to the basement. I decided that if I did not look into the dark corner of the earthen floor basement where the coal bin and furnace stood, I would be safe from the boogeyman. Besides, I had heard that God would take care of those who were trying to do good deeds.

Overcoming my fear, I filled the wringer washer with cold water. I had watched my mother wash clothes and knew how to use the machine. I thought she could hang the clothes outside when she came home. I guess I wasn't fully aware of how much care she took to feed each piece of clothing through the wringer one by one. I knew that sometimes if something got caught, she would hit the release to pop the rollers that wrung the water from the clothes. I had washed the clothes and began to rinse them when a sheet became stuck between the rollers. I hit the release with my left hand, but too late to stop the splitting of my right hand between the third and fourth fingers. Luckily, Mom had just come into the house as I screamed in pain. My cousin, Needie Gantt, who had just brought my mother home, drove us to the hospital with my hand wrapped in a blood-soaked towel. I still remember the pain-deadening, semi circular needle and six stitches, whose scars I still carry as a reminder of why washing clothes is today one of my least favorite activities.

We lived with Nannie, I think, until I was about ten years old. Despite the laundry incident, I have wonderful memories. There were no trees in front of Nannie's house, but in her back yard, between the house and the Kalamazoo River, were a number of peach trees that I imagined were protected by a snake-infested, grassy orchard. Not long before, Uncle Henry had chopped the head of a rattlesnake that ventured into the orchard from the river.

I missed seeing my Ann Street friends every day, but my other close childhood friend, Donna Jean Davidson, lived just across the bridge on the other side of the Kalamazoo River. Donna, the twins and I went to Sunday school together. We went on daring adventures as we played in my backyard wilderness—Donna daring me to cross the tall grass to pick a peach for each of us when Nannie wasn't looking. Those sweet, juicy peaches were and are the best I have ever eaten.

I remembered, as we stood on the Kalamazoo River Bridge, watching the water as it moved so freely along, we fantasized about traveling the world. We waved to our imaginary friends on the shore.

Donna and I walked across the bridge between our two homes—back and forth several times—sharing our dreams for the future. Donna was going to be a famous baton twirler, while I would be an equally famous ice skater. Our parents knew each other from church and lodge activities. We often convinced them to take us to the park across from the downtown. Sometimes we jumped rope to rhymes:

If you're black, stay back. If you're white, you're all right. If you're brown, stick around.

Dad called me into the house in a stern voice and said, "That is not a good poem," so Donna and I changed to the chant, "Donna and Charles under the tree, K-I-S-S-I-N-G. First comes love, then comes marriage, then comes Donna with a baby carriage."

Donna and I continued a banter that we started as little girls—we would

The Thompson twins, Donna and Beverly; me and June; and an unidentified little boy. The twins and I lived in sight of each other's houses on Ann Street, but we were too young to leave out houses without permission so we rode our tricycles up and down the street as far as we were allowed, laughing and calling to each other.

We never needed a reason to have a picnic or party. Left to right: me when they called me Ruth Elaine, Donna Jean, Rosemary Pearson and Shirley Gray. Shirley unfortunately died young.

ask, "Where have you been and where are you going?" and answer, "Learning to take care of my ash. Trying to get myself together to find out who I am and where I am going."

Pictured left to right: Cousin Robert, his daughter and grandson. Robert was one of several children of my dad's brother, William, from Detroit. Occasionally, the family drove down to visit us and play cards when we lived on Center Street in Albion.

A New Home

Maybe one of the memories of my mother that best serves me today is the grit she had—her determination to take care of her family. She decided that we needed a house of our own. She cleaned homes and worked at various times as a cook for the Albion College men's dorm. She worked in the homes of the people who owned the *Albion Evening Recorder,* the president of the only Albion bank, and for the wife of our family doctor, who provided excellent references to other white families, including the president of Albion College.

One day, Mother took me, June, Bob and Bill to see the house she had purchased at 619 Center Street. She was excited and shared her dreams with us. We were not as impressed as Mother was. We saw the house as it was. Mother saw the house as she planned it. Dad was in the sanitarium again, as he was off and on until I was about seventeen years old. That year, Dad had a lung removed, the first such operations performed by the University of Michigan medical team. I am not sure Dad was fully aware that Mom planned to buy a house when she did. He forbade her to go into debt, but that had no effect on Mom, who had determined that we required a home of our own. My dad reluctantly signed the papers for the mortgage only because in those days a woman could not get a loan on her own—certainly not a Negro woman.

She was conscientious about making payments and had excellent credit. After I left home, she would send my brother Bob to make the payments in person when she got paid. He recalls the anger he felt when he gave the money to the loan clerk at Household Finance, who admonished him in front of other customers about *slovenliness,* a common adjective assigned by whites to many Negroes. No matter how many payments Bob made, the principal never seemed to go down. We children believe our house was paid many times over to the lenders who engaged in predatory high-interest lending practices.

Both my mother and father made their dreams a reality through hard work and creativity. I remember when we looked at the Center Street house the first time, hearing Mom share her dreams, we looked at each other and exclaimed, "Yeah, right."

Mom made an agreement with the college to provide meals for the Negro college students who had been recruited to play football and live in the dormitory, but were not allowed to eat in the college dining rooms. Some of those young football players, among them Arnold Pinkney, whom I was to meet seven years later in Cleveland, would help my mother stoke the coal furnace in the dirt-floor basement at 619 West Center Street.

The size of this house seemed three times larger than Eaton Street. The four first-floor rooms seemed much larger. We children were not as happy, particularly with the toilet sitting in the open on the second floor. The attic storage area was at one end of this upstairs room.

Mom put us all to work and, within a few days, we had eliminated the grime. Although we were not aware at the time, I believe that Mom bartered work for remodeling and repairs. She also gained sympathy and respect from people who recognized her devotion to her family.

Mom assigned our places and daily chores. Bob and Bill were to sleep in a bed on one side of the second-floor room, while June and I would be in a bed on the other side of the room. A curtain would separate us. First, Mom found a room divider to put in front of the toilet we called "the bucket on the floor." We kids first grumbled, but then giggled as we thought about the tricks we might play on someone using that "bucket." Within a few weeks, a carpenter came to enclose the "bathroom" and build a wall between the two rooms. Closets were built in each room and a lock was put on the girls' side of the door.

My job was to make lunch for my siblings—thus prompting a joke about my making six sandwiches from a single can of potted meat. These cans were the size of the smallest can of tuna. As I grew older and went to high school, homework became the priority and I no longer had as many household chores. I went to work at the age of thirteen in white homes to earn extra money for personal needs and to begin saving for college.

Downstairs, the front was divided into two rooms: a bedroom and living room. The narrow windows were traded out for larger ones, including a picture window. The kitchen was in the back of the living room. Slowly, Mom bought blinds and curtains for all the windows and began to modernize the kitchen. Other workers came and built a bathroom onto the back of the kitchen and enclosed the elongated back porch so that Mom could set up her ironing board. The kitchen abutted the one bedroom on the first floor and was long enough to include the washing

Me in front of the family living room/dining room at 619 Center Street after much renovation. Left to right: Bob Jr., June, Mother, Bill and little Rodney in the foreground.

machine since the dirt-floor basement in this house was only large enough for the coal-fired furnace. Eventually, the house was complete—a kitchen/dining room, a full and half bathroom, an enclosed porch, two bedrooms upstairs and two bedrooms downstairs. A garage was a bonus. Mother was continuously redecorating and moving walls, a talent that June seems to have inherited from her.

Dad was really surprised when he saw the house Mother bought. I could tell Dad was excited because whenever he tried to hold back a smile, the dimple on the right side of his face appeared and the twinkle in his eyes betrayed his nonchalance. I think Dad struggled over the years between pride that his wife was so ingenious and more than a little hurt that he was not the provider he believed men should be.

Within a year of moving to 619 Center Street, Uncle Henry died and Nannie, and my aunt and godmother Lelia, moved three doors away from us. The Holland family was the first Negro family to buy a house on Center Street. There were some white families who were not thrilled to have us there. Some of them gathered in front of our house and threatened to burn the house down. My brothers Bob and Bill seem to remember this incident as including a burning cross, but I do not recall that. My father happened to be home from the sanitarium then. I remember him threatening to get his gun, which I do not remember him having. That was enough to disperse the crowd, and our lives went on without looking back or dwelling on that incident. In my life's walk, I have met others who had similar experiences, but they allowed themselves to internalize their anger, which grew to be a constant burden throughout their lives.

Mom and Dad Holland were very surprised by the 40th wedding anniversary party the children threw for them.

Charles and Geneva Smith were a big part of my neighborhood. We could see their house from our own. Charles was the Lewis Street Chapel A.M.E. Church Sunday school superintendent in Albion, Michigan, where I grew up. This couple gave me a lot of TLC and loved to take me on Sunday drives through the park, where they would encourage me to sing at the top of my lungs. Mrs. Smith developed crippling arthritis soon after their marriage and they could not have children. I believe I filled that need, much to my joy. When I grew older, a dish of ice cream was always there for me. Though they did not have a piano, they were the first to notice that I could not pass one without touching it. They lived three houses from Mrs. Ferguson, the teacher I called Aunt Ruth, who also adopted and encouraged my education.

S. Albion

S. Dalrymple

W. Center

1. Mr. and Mrs. Charles Smith's house (Sunday School Supt.)
2. Cousin Alice's house
3. Aunt Idell Caswell's house (hairdresser and mother's friend)
4. Ferguson (Aunt Ruth's) house
5. Ms. Benjamine's house
6. To:
    – Uncle Buddy's Home & Garden
    – First Lewis Chapel A.M.E. Church
    – Mr. Sweet's barber shop
    – Pierson's Grocery Store
    – Gertrude Hawkins (first Sunday school teacher)
7. Classmate Margerie Meyers' (Morgan) house
8. Holland family home
9. Nannie and Leila's house
10. West Ward Public School—now Holland Park
11. New Lewis Chapel A.M.E.

I grew up in a close-knit neighborhood on Center Street.

Ethel Fleenor was my speech teacher and debate coach. She encouraged me to learn and to attend college. She came to see me receive my Honorary Doctorate from Albion College.

Trying My Wings at Albion College

My senior year was filled with debate and college-prep activities. In the state of Michigan, there were two major events for high school senior debaters and speakers: one was a debate contest between the two highest-ranked high school debate teams and the other was a speaking competition, sponsored by the *Detroit Free Press*. Before this contest, Mrs. Fleenor chose Peggy Taylor and me to compete in the state contest. Individual speakers were invited to the University of Michigan to participate in an elimination contest. Winners were awarded one of four scholarships. As I remember, there were more than a hundred participants. Only four students were finally selected for scholarship awards. The format included choosing a subject out of a basket and going off to write about it. The topic would be from *Newsweek, Time Magazine, New York Times* or *Washington Post*. Some of the articles could be related to the debate topic. Half to two-thirds of the contestants were eliminated by their writing before they got to the panel for that year. I read *Vital Speeches, Fortune Magazine* and a few other expanded readings. The idea was that we were to read, remember and learn to manipulate the information we took in. We could take our notes with us, but no magazines or resources. The final round involved eight contestants and only four would receive the scholarships. In that final round, we were to listen to the presentation of the person in front of us, refute their statements and respond with our own chosen statements based on the statements we pulled from a hat, in favor of what we chose. This round was a ranking round, as well. I came in second out of eight. We won among all the debaters in the state that year.

After the scholarship round, the *Detroit Free Press* did a spread about each of the winners of the scholarship. The reporter asked if I had time for romance and I replied that there is always time for romance. However, the headline that tried to convey how busy I was said in bold face: **No Time for Romance**. Not too embarrassing for a high school senior with a full social life!

The scholarship I was awarded in the speech contest could be used anywhere. I applied to about six colleges, all of which accepted me. The Albion scholarship offer was contingent on acceptance by me at a certain date. I made the decision to attend Albion the day before I heard from the Board of Regents that I had received the scholarship to the University of Michigan based on a test and application I made to the board. They held the scholarship for two years in the event that I would go to Albion for two years then to the University of Michigan.

The whole town celebrated my scholarship award and shared in my joy. The merchants in Albion presented me with the opportunities to celebrate my victory by choosing from their inventory *any* priced selection from their stock. The three gifts that stand out are luggage, a watch from the jewelry store and a black coat with red piping. Despite that celebrity celebration, it did not go to my head. I appreciated my town's celebration with me.

I know Mrs. Fleenor had a lot to do with getting the scholarship for me at Albion and one from the Methodist Women's groups who adopted me and sent $20 a month for all four years I attended. I could not help but feel there was some divine involvement there.

Moreover, since eighth grade, she had arranged for me to be adopted by and dine with the Dean Hall girls, a co-op house in which all the girls participated in their own cleaning, laundry, cooking, etc. at the college, which made my attendance there seamless. Other campus students had their cooking and the cleaning of common areas done for them, but they paid higher room and board costs.

I did not realize when I left for college that I was leaving home forever. I often reflect on the memories of Mom and Dad and the values I took with me when I left that kept with me into my adulthood. I remember sitting with my mother in the kitchen while she canned or ironed shirts for other people. I learned a lot of life's lessons from her as I asked questions. When I went away to college—though it was still in town— my roommate and I would call Mom and tell her we were hungry. Despite her long work days, she came over with fried chicken or pound cake.

I know I got my love of poetry from Dad. He used to start a line of poetry and wait for me to finish it. When he was home convalescing from the hospital, I would hear him recite a line—my cue to come to his bedside to hear him finish the poem. He would recite his favorite poems—serious, funny and inspirational ones. After he was a married adult and suffering the pain of a diseased lung, he memorized all the poems from the book *Best Loved Poems of the American People*. He told me memorization kept the pain away. He often shared these poems with me

Me with my Albion College debate team and Coach Aggertt in the center.

at night as a substitute for a bedtime story. My siblings slowly moved out of his room to go play. I stayed until mother said, "Ruth Elaine, it's time for you to go to bed." Two poems that he loved stand out in my memory: *Invictus* by William Ernest Henley and *If* by Rudyard Kipling. As I grew older and too busy as a teenager to sit at his feet, he would throw out a line of poetry such as "I have to live with myself, and so ..." He expected my answer. "I want to be fit for myself to know."

When I left for college, I left for good, but in my heart and mind I never left the lessons they instilled in me. Mom's advice has rung in my head all my life—"Be yourself."

My fondest memories of Albion College are those of learning, laughing and crying. Many of my memories are bittersweet ones, like the hours I spent weeping in Dr. Swan's office (head of the Sociology Department) when rejected by my writing teacher, Dr. Snow, who refused to give me any encouragement or suggestions in writing. D was the grade of the hour as far as she was concerned. I, who had never had a grade below A in high school English and writing, was devastated. Dr. Swan and Dr. Aggertt, my debate coach, were extremely supportive. Dr. Swan tried to buoy my spirits by deciding that I needed to be a sociologist among whose members I would undoubtedly be welcomed.

Another fond memory is my constant battles with Dean Wilder, whom I greatly respected. At her suggestion, I joined the American Association of University Women—AAUW—as soon as I was in a city that had one, even though I hated to come under her authority. Dean Wilder and I battled over many things, but one that stands out is her canceling my appearance to speak to a church conference audience of five thousand without first telling me. Of course, there was the little inconvenience that I was diagnosed with mononucleosis and confined to the infirmary. Another notable fight was about an honors report I wrote researching and analyzing the treatment of abandoned children by the State of Michigan. The governor requested a copy of the paper, but I was forbidden to give him a copy, as it would "look like" a private institution criticizing a public institution. One battle I won with her due to the diligence of Dr. Aggertt was that she felt it unseemly for a girl to travel overnight with the all-male debate team to Madison, Wisconsin, for speech contests. Joe Munk and I had been debate partners and friends during high school and through college. We had many adventures on that trip, which are too long to repeat.

In one memorable and stinging instance, the hotel Dr. Aggertt reserved refused to let me stay in a room because, the clerk said, "We don't allow colored here." The clerk followed with, "Unless she stays in your room." With great anger, we drove all night and, in spite of being tired, we simply threw water on our faces and met our first assigned contests. We won—and placed in every one, taking trophies back to Albion, which the dean applauded.

Some classes opened my mind in ways that would never allow narrowness of thought to really take permanent root in my life. Studying plant life in Botany class gave me an appreciation for the beauty of the earth and the sustaining power of plant life. I developed a firm belief in eternal life. Through Dr. Munk's philosophy classes, my mind was challenged and expanded. I often think about his statements about the necessity of working for world peace and our walking on the "precipice of the abyss." That class introduced me to a new discipline of thinking and expression, which, like debate, has been a cornerstone of my achievements and work. My piano class helped me realize that "world-class pianist" was not a part of my future, but being an appreciator and supporter of music prepared me to be a musician's wife.

I was obviously a favorite of Joe's father, Dr. Munk's. I often played the piano for Joe while he sang for his mother's missionary groups. One day, when Dr. Munk was speaking about the equality of all human beings, he was challenged by one student who asked, "How would you like it if your son married Ruth Holland?"

Dr. Munk replied, "I would be honored to have Ruth Holland as my daughter-in-law."

Dean Hall became my college residence. It was a cheaper place to live. It was rumored that Susanna Wesley Hall still had a donor's restrictive covenant, which did not allow Negro girls to live there.

My organizing of the "Independents" was working with non-Greeks to assure that unaffiliated students would have some place in the social scheme of things at Albion, especially homecoming. It was great to be a nominee for homecoming queen; however, the event organizers did not really include us non-Greek students. In discussions with Tom Brown, president of Goodrich House (the male counterpart of Dean Hall), we decided to petition the Hellenic Council for the inclusion of the Independents in the Queens Court and the Goodrich guys informed me I would be the candidate for the Independents. We didn't think I needed an escort for the game day, but the organizers pulled a black nonstudent spectator from the stands to bring me into the stadium. It was an embarrassing moment. But Perry Hawkins, the spectator, became a good friend and later in the school year, lent me his car to travel to interviews for teaching jobs. Perry disappeared on a trip to South America. Years later, I discovered that he was the nephew of my first Sunday School teacher, Gertrude Hawkins, and the brother of our lead singer in our youth choir at Lewis Chapel.

George Hawkins and his wife, Liz, would embrace and mentor our children when they visited Mom and Dad Holland and attended the "Albion Adventure" at Albion College. I never heard from Perry again.

Through Dean Hall, I met Sally Ball Holmes, my college roommate and lifelong friend. Dean Hall was a great normalizing experience. I had been "adopted" by Dean Hall girls as an eighth grader and therefore ate many Tuesday night meals in the dining room before coming to college. Like Wordsworth's *Daffodils,* I have memories of singing in the Dean Hall choir—*White Coral Bells, She Walks in Beauty* and *These Dean Hall Days Are Ours Forever* still bring me joy. Dean Hall was also notable for my learning to bake bread. Our house mother—a delightful, Scottish, easily embarrassed, lovable person—was the bread maker teacher. To this day, I enjoy baking bread. She had gorgeous white hair and fair skin, which often turned a shade of bright pink at our antics. One night, she knocked on the room door to inquire what the noise was about. We told her we were having an "unbirthday" party. She thought it wonderful that we would celebrate the birthday of the United Nations. Spring break-outs, serenades, playing bridge hands throughout finals by leaving unplayed hands face down when someone had to leave for a test, and coming in the back window of Dean Hall after curfew are also a few of my favorite memories.

Being surrounded by many of my high school acquaintances and friends, like Betty and Beverly Thompson, Charles Anderson, Joe Munk and Buddy Fox made the transition to college wonderfully comfortable. Seeing them and talking with them in the library or after classes, where we discussed and solved all the problems in the world, were special moments in a blessed life. Making new lifelong friends like Beth Munk, Sally Ball Holmes, Dorothy and Tom Lennox and Phyllis Harrison gave me a solid foundation to go to the next experiences in life after Albion. Phyllis Harrison's mother was instrumental in my being inducted into the prestigious Delta Sigma Theta African-American Sorority because she wanted Phyllis to become a sorority member and there had to be two members at a college. We were inducted into the Wayne State Chapter in 1955 and that affiliation has also become lifelong. Phyllis Harrison-Ross became a noted psychiatrist in New York City and became member of the New York State Commission of Correction and chair of the Medical Review Board.

Women were often encouraged to get a teaching certificate because employment opportunities were locked out in other fields. I accepted the challenge as a first step in my career ladder because of Ethel Fleenor. I majored in secondary education and sociology. My plan was to teach English for a year or two before going on to graduate school.

At the end of my junior year, I was called into the office by Dr. Thomas Carter, the dean of education. He told me he could not place me in a high school teaching position because of my color. He wanted me to change my major to elementary education. He didn't go into detail and I was too shocked to ask questions. My heart sank. I was planning to take music, art and philosophy, or other electives in my senior year. He insisted that I change my major *and* add additional classes, including special education and elementary teaching methods.

On the chance that Dean Carter was right about placement only in elementary teaching positions, I took a job at a children's summer camp in Ohio. I signed on as head counselor to a group of eight-to-ten-year-olds whose wealthy parents usually left their children at camp for the entire summer while they went off on vacations.

Each group of forty children was supervised by eight counselors and one head counselor. This was indeed a good choice for a summer job for me to explore my career options, for it was here at camp that I learned that my love of children below the age of adult reasoning was limited to one child at a time.

We had children who had special psychological problems and all of the "finding out who I am" issues of preadolescence. The camp directors did not seem in the least to understand what life in the cabins was really like for each counselor who lived with these kids. I remember one child who seemed not to relate to any of us. She talked continuously about her conversations with imaginary friends who lived in the trees. She insisted on visiting these friends in the forest after midnight. And, of course, who had to be on alert for these little escapes or retrieve her if she did escape my necessarily light sleep?

The camp directors, of course, were trying not to disturb the parents of the children who had left them at camp while they traveled in Europe. For me, this work experience strengthened my determination to teach high school.

Donna Davidson and daughter Tammie in a Catholic church in Cleveland, Ohio, where Donna served as a minister.

Out Into the World

I graduated cum laude from Albion College in 1956. Three months before graduation, I began the exciting process of job hunting. We all wondered where our searches would take us and what adventures we would have in our careers.

I soon found the process quite frustrating. I applied and interviewed all over Michigan, but kept hearing "We don't have any Negro teachers and we don't believe the white parents of our district would accept a Negro." Even my hometown high school rejected me. Although I had performed my student teaching assignment there in Mrs. Fleenor's debate class and had received A's from the college supervisor and Mrs. Fleenor, I did not even get a call back in response to my application.

One school in Eaton, Michigan, offered to modify its hesitation to hire a Negro by saying they would hire me as the elementary school librarian. If that worked out—meaning if no one complained about my color—when there was an "appropriate" opening in elementary school, they would try me out as a temporary teacher. You can imagine the frustration and flash of anger that I held inside because I knew I could not show it in the interview.

I finally landed a junior high teaching job in Cleveland at 98th Street and Superior Avenue. Complicating my decision to take this position after what seemed like a long search was the offer of a full scholarship to do post graduate work in Negro history at Fisk University under a professor friend of my Albion philosophy professor, Dr. Arthur Munk. When I decided to take the Cleveland teaching position, this offer was extended two years. I had several other offers to do graduate work, including a Woodrow Wilson Fellowship. I passed up all of them for the time being. My best childhood friend, Donna Davidson, had also moved to Cleveland and was expecting her first baby. Caught up in the direction of my life in Cleveland, I never followed up again on these offers.

I had a hesitation—maybe even a fear—about the independence that I suddenly had as a young woman. But I looked forward to the freedom and independence. I wasn't looking to date or marry while I was in college—maybe because I was writing to a young man whom I thought someday I would marry, but hoped Cleveland would offer new social opportunities and maybe the right person.

Though I didn't realize it at the time, working in Cleveland drew me into a circle I have remained a part of my whole life. It was in Cleveland that Arnold Pinkney, who had eaten at my mother's table as an Albion College student, invited me to parties at the Stokes brothers' home. There were several groups at these parties—some caught up in the love of their date, some just having a great time, and me in the group that talked about serious issues and how we would change the world someday. There were some international students, fraternity brothers and others from Morehouse College in Atlanta, and new college graduates who came to live in Cleveland. Some of the party-goers were there just to listen to cool jazz.

Several of the people at these parties became elected officials, including Louis Stokes, who went to Congress, and Carl, who became the first black mayor of Cleveland. Arnold Pinkney married one of the Thompson twins from Ann Street and became the national chair of Jesse Jackson's run for the United States president. Jackson was the first African-American candidate to enter and win delegate votes for the Democratic nomination for president.

I became a member of the Antioch Baptist Church on the corner of Cedar Avenue and 89th Street. There, I met Percy Scott, the program director of the YMCA on Cedar Avenue. The Y in Albion was for whites only, so their activities and offerings were a mystery to me. It would remain so in Cleveland, as well, as the Cedar Y was designated the "Negro" Y.

Percy was in my Sunday School class at Antioch Baptist Church. Rose McKee was also one of my social buddies from Antioch Church. One day, Percy invited young people to become program volunteers at the Y in trade for free classes. I took him up on the offer, not only to volunteer in my new community, but because I had been teaching in Cleveland for only a year and it was a good way to meet more people.

And I did. I met the most important person in my life, yet at the time I didn't realize it. One Thursday evening after my bridge class, I was passing by Percy's office when I caught a very animated shadow of "Percy" sitting at his desk talking with someone. It turned out that I knew the other man as Rayfer Johnson, whom I had known since our teen years.

I was embarrassed when "Percy" set me straight in the resonating bass voice I have come to know so well, "I'm Bill Scott, not Percy Scott."

That unnerved me enough that I completely ignored Bill and started reminiscing with Rayfer. I had not seen him since high school.

Rayfer was one of a caravan of young boys and girls who traveled from Flint to Albion, Michigan because Albion had a skating rink that opened its doors to Negroes on Thursday evenings. The youth also took part in church and recreational activities, including street dances alongside the inferior, segregated West Ward Elementary School.

My Cleveland friend, Rose Aiken (McKee). Rose and I met Cleveland public tennis courts early in my teaching career and have become constant friends. She introduced me to Antioch Baptist Church and its Young Adult Club. Her husband Bill McKee graduated from Rochester Colgate Divinity School. We are Godparents to their younger son Randy.

Teaching Becomes a Lifelong Obsession

After a challenging search, facing much discrimination, I did manage to find housing in Cleveland a short distance from where I would be teaching, going to church, dancing at Karamu House and volunteering at the YMCA. After her graduation, my sister June came to live with me until she found an apartment.

On one of my first bus trips to school, I was asked by Negro bus riders where I was going all dressed up. They were surprised when I told them I was teaching school. They didn't know there were Negro high school teachers in core subjects. They were intrigued by my stories of job hunting. They seemed to share a vicarious pride in my getting an appointment to my first teaching assignment. I know our conversations gave them encouragement and validated my sense that my life could serve as a role model. I wish I could have given these young people more.

I taught at the junior high on 98th and Superior for one year in seventh through ninth grades. The school was in a very poor neighborhood. In one of my ninth grade classes, students were over-aged, out of control, undisciplined and unfocused. If you've ever seen the movie *Up the Down Staircase,* then you've seen my students. The maintenance of the building was minimal at best. Supplies were poor to none. I loved to read and teach literature, so I went to the director of English and asked for the books I would be using in the coming year. He looked at me somewhat astonished. They did not require class plans then and were not accustomed to this kind of teacher preparedness.

There were no assemblies planned at the school, so I asked the principal if I could plan some student-participation assemblies. He was as astonished as the English Department head, but I forged ahead. I produced student-led assemblies for the major holidays and invited other English teachers to join me with some success. During the last period of the day I led a school choir.

The students performed assemblies and traveled with me on public transportation to other schools where they performed. City busses would not carry more than three students at a time during the school day, so I assigned a lead student to keep the other students together on the next bus. I was a little apprehensive, but the trips were successful. The faith I had in the students was rewarded.

I loved my classes, but learned from one of my student leaders that if I gave the students choices, they believed that meant that I did not know what to do next. They were not accustomed to participating in their own education, but were perhaps all too accustomed to teachers not knowing what to do next.

I used to give my students a speech at the beginning of the year that went something like: "I believe all of you have some wonderful talents and ideas inside of you. You and I are going on an adventure this year to discover that talent. After all, it is scientifically proven that we only use one 100th of our brain power, so no matter what others may have told you, I expect you to do well. I will give you the grades you deserve with the hard work you will do in this class."

There were some groans when they heard "hard work," but for the most part, this statement seemed to set a stage for students to try to do good work. This always kicked off a conversation about the "what ifs" and the discouraging statements made by other people that dampened the spirits and self esteem of these students. One thing I learned early in my teaching career is that students *do* want structure and expectations spelled out for them, and they will work hard to meet them. I believe that structure is one reason why some charter and private schools outperform some public schools. When public schools relaxed discipline, then tried to reinstate it, they found it challenging and often unsuccessful.

I certainly did have some discipline challenges. In one class, the boys outweighed me by at least one hundred pounds. It was obvious even to these overgrown ninth-graders that they were a year or two behind. These students had run other teachers out of the classroom and they saw me as just the next mini-challenge to their bored intellect.

One day, as I began to teach, a student began a whistle that grew louder and louder only to cease as I turned around. Another time I turned from writing on the blackboard to find the floor littered with papers like a sudden snowfall. I struggled through the first day, trying to neither scream nor run out of the room. The nearby male shop teacher, a friend indeed, stepped into the room a few times to quiet the boys down. As an aside, he told me, "It's going to be you or them."

"What can I do?" I asked.

"Use the paddle," he strongly advised.

This shop teacher's class was in the basement across from my class. He took me under his wing early on, made a paddle for me and suggested that I keep it in sight. One day, I did take his advice and used the paddle. The next day, when the boys again became disruptive, I took them out of the room one by one and told them to bend over. They looked at me and smirked, "You can't hurt me!"

Guess what?

As each boy bent over somewhat obediently, but still defiant, I hit them once as hard as I could with the paddle. By the time I finished that day, the room was quiet and attentive. I hated to resort to what I considered violence, but I promised early in my career to be an instrument of God's peace and I had prayed for an answer. I believe God sent that shop teacher as a messenger with a custom-made instrument of peace.

That discipline did not suit me well but, driven to desperation, I used it and it did get the class back under control. The shop teacher came back to congratulate me and I did not find it necessary to use it again. I had not heard at that time about the student in another school who shot the teacher who tried to paddle him.

I learned that it is much easier to ease up on the students after you lay down the law than to try to lay down the law after being too easy. I also think this discipline worked because I did not embarrass the students in front of their classmates.

I worked with students in my four classes by assigning them to write an essay from the best line of each student's paper. They learned to critique papers and determine grades. When I found a student who struggled, I worked with that student while the other students worked on their assignments.

I had a challenging year, but I honed my teaching skills and learned the need for discipline. It came as a surprise to me when my supervisor came to me with the news that the principal would not rehire me for the next year. Apparently, the extra work I did with assemblies, choir and class trips did not impress him. He said that I was a know-it-all since I was a new teacher who did not ask his advice or send him ill-mannered students. He was right about that. I did not seek his advice or send him students. My limited contact with this principal was hearing his daily "pronouncements" on the PA system: "Hear this. Now hear this ..."

I was pretty apprehensive about seeing my supervisor in the downtown office. I was proud of my accomplishments and those of my students who wrote many notes saying thank you and, "I hope I have you next year."

The supervisor expressed disappointment in me, but conceded the principal was a hard nut to crack. We discussed my first year and the supervisor's inclination to send me to an all-black school that had a reputation for convincing teachers to leave the field. I graciously declined his offer.

A few days later, he called to say a principal whose daughter was a debater saw my resume and told the supervisor, "I want that teacher at Charles Elliott School. "If she is a debater, I know she can teach." The principal at this school, on the border of Cleveland and Euclid, Ohio, was as supportive as the previous one had been unsupportive. At the end of that year, he recommended that I be promoted to high school. It was here at Charles Elliott School that I perfected my first-day speech.

One of my classes was a special-education class. One day, I arrived early and stood in the hallway unnoticed as a student stood in front of the class and said, "I know we're going to have a test, an' if we do well, we'll have to work harder so, everybody, let's fail the test."

I did not take the student's remarks personally, nor did I challenge her. Instead, I created an optimal learning environment and we became the best of learning buddies.

In my third year I landed a position at the Glenville High School in the heart of Cleveland. There I was surrounded with supportive teaching colleagues including Bill Miller, a Negro concert pianist who performed with the Cleveland Symphony.

Drawing from both middle- and low-income students, I was assigned to teach some of the college prep classes the school had become known for. I was assigned to teach the over-aged students who were getting their last shot at high school graduation. Though older like the undisciplined students I taught in my first year, these students presented a different challenge. Unlike most students in this college prep school, my students told me their most pressing need was getting a job when they graduate.

I developed a work-training program with local stores and small industries before work internship programs were popular. I was enrolled at the time in graduate school at Kent State University majoring in counseling with a minor in reading. I created materials for older students to read after finding that most reading materials were for young children first learning to read. If I had remained in Cleveland another few years, I would have followed up with those students and perhaps marketed those needed materials.

One of my senior classes had a large number of Negro students who didn't buy my optimism about developing their abilities and having a successful career. They had internalized the lack of success they saw in the lives of their parents and other relatives as they worked in the white metropolis. Some students told me of relatives who had a college degree yet worked for the U.S. Post Office. When I shared my personal story of success in landing a job teaching in high school as I had planned, most students were not convinced that they, too, would succeed. I do not know if my enthusiasm for their future ever took hold, but my enthusiasm for learning was visible in the papers they wrote.

One white student challenged me by refusing to do his assignments, saying he intended to be a Nazi and would not read or write anything that was not on that subject. He gave rip-roaring speeches that captivated his classmates, but I gave him D's. He was a bright kid who taxed my imagination as I tried to find a hook to stretch his learning.

He complained about the D's. "Why?" he would cry.

"Because you didn't fulfill the assignment," I responded.

"But you agree I am a great speaker, don't you?" he insisted.

"Not if you lose the audience because they came to hear something else," I answered.

I really prayed over this one and scratched my head trying to engage him in an argument in my area of expertise. When this student accused me of being a Christian, I knew I had him. I decided, since he was so enthralled with Hitler, to raise questions about the philosophers Hegel and Kant from whose philosophies Hitler drew some of his own ideas.

To his charge that I am a Christian, I responded, "Yes, I am."

He responded, "Then you are weak and should not be given anything— work or pay."

I answered with a defusing blow to his frail sense of superiority, "Hegel and Kant put Christ in the Superman category—those who should be given power."

"Where did you get that?" he asked.

"Look it up," I answered.

I had no more challenges from this student, but I have often wondered what became of him and several other students I taught in my early years.

Bill Scott and I had been seeing each other since my first year teaching in Cleveland. He was attending SUNY Fredonia, majoring in music. He often rode the train to Cleveland supposedly, at first, to see his brother. He wrote me boxes of letters that I still treasure fifty years later. I'll let him tell you his part of the story.

In the Right Place at the Right Time
—Bill's Story

After my stint in the Army, I scheduled a re-admission interview at SUNY Fredonia. I was discharged from Fort Leonard Wood in St. Louis, Missouri, and with a little time to pass before my interview, I scheduled a few stops—first in Cincinnati, Ohio, to visit my great aunt for a few days and then on to Cleveland to visit my brother. Little did I know that the stop meant to pass some idle time before my interview became an important life-changing visit. As Ruth said earlier, my brother worked at the YMCA in Cleveland a few blocks away from the church where he came to know Ruth. One day, when I walked over to visit him, I saw this wonderful young lady. She came to volunteer and, thinking I was my brother Percy, she introduced herself and turned to the long-lost friend I was talking to in my brother's office, pretty much ignoring me.

That Sunday at church, this same young lady made an announcement regarding a Memorial Day event being sponsored by the young adult members of the church. Being "shy and retiring," I asked her if I could go to the picnic with her. Her response wasn't quite what I had in mind. She said I could meet the main part of the group at the church and someone would give me a ride. Somehow in the midst of the conversation, her phone number came into my possession, so I called her during the week and "badgered" her into letting me go with her and another friend. They were meeting at her apartment, and so I met them there.

I was introduced to Ruth's friend, Rosemary Aiken McKee, who said to me, "You two should have something to talk about since Chuck Perry, Rosemary's boyfriend, just got out of the Army, too."

As the ladies were preparing some foods in the kitchen, we got to know each other. Talk about a small world. He had been in the All Army Talent show that toured the Army bases entertaining troops. He had performed at Fort Leonard Wood. We were in the same group that went out on the town after the show!

I enjoyed the rest of the day. I heard later that Ruth did also. Several dates later, before I left Cleveland, I asked if she would write to me and she promised to answer every letter I wrote to her. That fall, I returned to my studies a junior at Fredonia. I started interviewing in my senior year and, after being rejected by *every* school I applied to, my advisor suggested that perhaps my race was my obstacle. Strangely, that had not occurred to me, but I accepted that that could be a possibility. When my senior year ended, I was still interviewing when I returned to summer camp as Assistant Director. I soon received an invitation to interview at Delevan, New York, so I caught a plane to Buffalo and rented a car. Delevan was so small, I drove right through the town, since the only traffic light was green. I had a good interview. The interviewing principal asked me, "How do you feel about teaching in a school where there are no Negro children?"

I answered, "My certification is to teach children."

Fortunately, I was offered the position. About ten days later, I received a phone call from the principal to return to Delevan to meet the entire school board. I traveled again from camp to Delevan to meet with the board for only about ten minutes. Much later, while teaching at Delevan, I learned that there had been meetings, sermons and a student petition supporting my appointment.

Many of the new teachers were planning to live in the boarding house in Delevan. I preferred a little more private space, so I spoke to the principal, who told me of a one-bedroom furnished apartment in walking distance of the school that would be ready in time for school. In late August, the principal called to tell me the apartment would not be ready after all, but I could live temporarily with the bachelor Methodist minister in the parsonage.

I contacted the minister and learned that, on the day I would arrive, he would be with a youth group for a Labor Day picnic. He would leave the door open, food in the refrigerator and directions to my guest room. He added that I should not be surprised when the "girls" bounded upstairs with me. The girls were a pair of mixed boxers!

That minister, the Rev. Earl Houck, and I became great friends. He was a jazz fan. His favorite singer was Billie Holiday. I used to tease him that one night, someone would check into town in dire need of a minister and would be directed to the parsonage, where they would hear the strains of Billie Holiday as they climbed the porch steps. We remained friends until his death. Our first child carries his first name as his middle name and he is his godfather. His first child carries Ruth's first name as her middle name and we are her godparents.

Earl and Marilyn Houck at camp. Earl was the minister Bill stayed with when he took his first teaching position in Delevan. Our son Greg carries Earl's name as his middle name and Earl is his godfather. Their daughter Marcy's middle name is Ruth. Earl was eventually assigned to Niagara Falls, New York, then to Washington state. We remained in touch over the years. They came to visit several times over the twelve years we worked at the St. John's summer camp in the Catskills.

My apartment was finally ready. It was a small and on the second floor opposite the son and daughter-in-law of the owner of the house; they lived on the first floor. Bill and Pat Waring became good friends. He was a physicist who had been sent to college because he was the oldest son. He had no intention of coming back home to run the family farm appliance business, but when his father passed away, Bill returned home. Compared to today's banking practices, he was a terrible businessman. He made loans to farmers who couldn't pay until the harvest came in. If they couldn't make timely payments he was p-a-t-i-e-n-t.

In the meantime, Ruth and I were successfully carrying on a long-distance relationship. Her insistence that I write if I wanted to get letters from her prompted me, and I also saw her when I went to Cleveland to "visit my brother." That summer, after my first year teaching in Delevan, Ruth planned to visit New York City. My father worked there, so I gave her directions to meet with him. He asked my mother to call Ruth to invite her to their home in White Plains. I learned they really hit it off, though I heard they were not sure whether Ruth was interested in me or my brother Percy.

St. John's Summer Camp Director Jane Porter, on the left with Mrs. Billy, the camp cook. My Bill was program director and later assistant camp director. His duties included programs, human resources, supervision of camp counselors, assistant health director and "Jack of all Trades," but Bill often helped Mrs. Billy too. I was dorm director before I married and later "assistant to Bill." What I learned watching Bill was that he was a morale builder and great helping hand. The Church of Saint John the Divine in New York City owned the camp and provided personal support, collecting clothing for the children brought to the camp. Many had only the clothes on their backs. The camp was a magical place that grew out of the surrounding forest just west of the town of Haverstraw in the village of Tomkins Cove, New York, at the foot of Bear Mountain. Some children grew up to become staff members or brought their own children. One of the women who came to our wedding anniversary celebration had been to camp. I spent most of my free time at the Gatehouse with Bill if his time off coincided with mine. I occasionally went alone to the chapel.

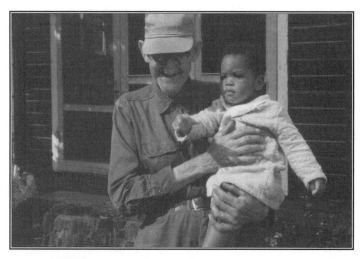

Alex the handyman and his helper, our son Greg.

I returned to camp the next summer. The head of the girls' section accidentally broke her leg and had to break her contract. The director asked during a pre-camp meeting if any of us knew someone who could fill in for this staff person. I mentioned my friend Ruth, of course. She was interviewed and hired. A few years later, I learned from Ruth that she expected that someday I would take her to Africa, since it had been her dream before she took the camp job.

When we were together, we discussed generally how many children we hoped to have and what our family values were. Our relationship grew more serious as the year came to a close. That Christmas, in 1960, I proposed to her and presented her with a ring. We kept the engagement a secret from most of the fellow staffers at camp that summer, as business and personal lives were not to be mixed. Of course, a few staffers who were friends and close to the director did know our secret. The Sunday before Ruth left to go back to Michigan to prepare for the wedding, our friends gave us a gift and wonderful party.

We were married in Michigan. I had little to do with the planning, but Ruth did a wonderful job. All I had to do was show up. We had a honeymoon in a nicely appointed cabin at Cape Cod. We walked to restaurants and shopping. We traveled to White Plains for a second reception. We were now all family!

With the wedding behind us, we returned to Delevan as Mr. and Mrs. Bill Scott. There had been an announcement and photograph in the small weekly paper, so it was not a complete surprise to people there. Strangely though, people thought Ruth was from Buffalo because I spent so much time there, as it was the nearest major city. Every other week, I used to take the bus into Buffalo and check into a hotel. I took my meals in the dining room at the hotel and returned to my room for a night of television. The next morning, I got a haircut, caught a movie and took the bus back to Delevan on Saturday afternoon.

Our lives were coming together. Ruth got an interview for a teaching position in West Valley. She got the job and later that winter, in order to give the principal a "heads up," informed him that she was expecting a child.

Surprisingly, he gave her notice that she would have to leave almost immediately saying "our children are used to seeing cows pregnant ... not their teachers."

Bill's parents, Mom and Dad Scott at our wedding.

I could not have had more wonderful in-laws than Mom and Dad Scott. Little did I know that when I enjoyed that Sunday invitation to dinner before Bill and I were actually dating, this was a foundation for feeding a thirst of fun and family that I did not even know I had. We have looked back on those days with fondness over the years. It does not see possible that they are no longer with us. Perhaps because we hear them in the laughter and see them in the perseverance of our children.

My bridesmaids and I shared many wonderful adventures growing up, but none more precious than on my wedding day. Left to right, Rosemary Pearson, Vern Kinsey, sister June, me, Donna Davidson, flower girl Renee Gant, Beverly Thompson and Sally Holmes. Vern became a journalist, assistant attorney general in the state of Michigan and, finally, a U.S. Magistrate Judge in Ohio. Donna became a minister in the Catholic church. Beverly became a teacher and married a pro football star. Sally was my college roommate and remains my friend. Sally did her student teaching in my brother Rodney's class.

Maybe it was the times or that hindsight is 20/20. In retrospect, we could have filed a lawsuit for his response, and remarks were both racist and sexist. I don't know if it had any influence on the principal's response, but Ruth was the only Negro on the staff. It is not our nature to create a stir, so we passed on this event in our lives, but it still comes back to us like an unaddressed issue.

I learned from the instrument teacher at my school that we had both been active in the Student Christian Association at Fredonia. We were also active in NYS Student Baptist Movement and the Fredonia Baptist Church. My friend Clarence Zeeches told his Baptist minister that I was hired to teach music and was a voice major. Maybe I could teach Sunday School there. That minister did not warm up to the proposal or share my friend's enthusiasm. Since there were no Negroes in Delevan before I arrived, he had no way of knowing that in this very fundamental Baptist Church I, as a Negro, would not be embraced.

Ruth and I became members of the Delevan United Methodist Church. The Methodist minister, very considerately, told me that even though I lived in the Methodist parsonage at the time I joined the church, he would understand if I wanted to join the Baptist Church because he knew I had a Baptist background.

During my first year teaching at Delevan, I was approached by the nearby Chaffee Baptist Church to become choir director. The search committee interviewed me and I accepted the position even while I was singing in the Methodist choir the same morning. It was a great offer and it worked well.

We became active in the community. I was invited to join the local Kiwanis and Ruth joined the local Knowledge Seekers (KS), known also as the Women's Intelligence Book Club. The Kiwanis met at one of the local restaurants.

Now that I was married, I wanted to stop traveling all the way to Buffalo to have my hair cut. One afternoon on my way home from school, I stopped at the Delevan barber shop and asked for a haircut. The rather flustered barber responded that he had never cut Negro hair before but he was willing to try. I asked for a hand mirror and told him not to cut anything that I did not tell him to cut. It took a while, but he learned to cut my hair and I had a *local* barber.

Mavis (second from left) and Steve Smith (third from left). Steve was the vice principal at Delevan Machias Central School. Mavis was a teacher for Cornell Extension in home economics in Yorkshire, New York. We became good friends and she was a fellow member of the book club called KS (the Knowledge Seekers.) She encouraged me to become one of the advisors to Governor Rockefeller on rural affairs.

Now that Ruth and I were parents with our son Greg, we decided that the one-bedroom apartment was not large enough. We looked for a short time before we realized we would not be happy in an apartment, but we didn't think we could afford a house. It was evident that what we wanted could not be found in the older houses we saw for sale.

Someone referred us to a new home builder who said he had a new house for sale right in town. Maybe we should take a look at that. He thought we could make a deal. We looked despite having no down payment. Surprisingly, we came to an agreement.

I went to the only bank in town to apply for a mortgage because that officer was easy to work with when I needed a car loan earlier. That banker simply asked, "Do you like the car? Who are you buying from? How much is he asking? Okay, we can do it."

I sat down at the bank with the same loan officer who approved my car loan. This time, though, I was going for a much larger loan and had no down payment. The bank could only do a loan for two-thirds of the direct mortgage. *Then* came the miracle! Even though I was a contract teacher and my tenure would not come up for another two years, the bank officer gave us a second mortgage to cover the down payment.

The builder confided to Ruth and I that he had discussed the potential sale with his monsignor. Ruth and I had integrated the town and Catholics, more than we, were having difficulty being accepted as equals to Protestants in this small town and adjusting to this new life.

The bank house closing made the miracle a reality. We were now the owners of a three-bedroom, single-story house with a full basement on a three-quarter-acre lot. The house had a tiled kitchen with a new electric stove, dining area and modern full bathroom.

We purchased this home for $12,000. The seller agreed to the second mortgage and commented that he didn't like a lot of paperwork. He allowed us to make a single payment to cover both the first and second mortgages. The single lawyer who represented all of us—the seller, the bank, and Ruth and I as buyers—said, "Have you got a dollar in your pocket so we can have an exchange of cash to seal the contract?"

I gave him a dollar that he passed to the seller.

We signed the contract and shook hands. We were now homeowners!

After I finished graduate school, we had our second child, June. I expected to be present at her birth as I was for Greg's; however, even though we calculated that it was safe to go to the music conference, I was away when I got the call that Ruth was in labor. I impatiently waited for daylight, then drove as fast as the law allowed through the snow some 400 miles to get to the hospital. By the time I got there, our daughter was born.

The Delevan School District merged with the neighboring district, doubling its size. I applied for the new position of music department chairman. I had completed my master's degree and had been active professionally, not only in the county, but also in the state music activities. Our students from Delevan schools had been in the all-county performing groups and the NYSSMA Sectional festival groups. Two of our students were accepted into the state-wide performing

Bill's Madison High School choir performing at Rochester City Hall at Christmas.

organizations. Personally I had been president of the County Music Teachers' Association, zone chair of the State Teachers Music Division. The principal who hired me was promoted to superintendent of the new district. He believed appointments such as the new department chair should be made by the local principal. So the new high school principal appointed a man who had been a teacher only four years and was not involved in neither county- nor state-level music associations.

I confided in the new superintendent, George Crawford, that I was seeking a position elsewhere. He said he was aware of that since he had received requests for recommendations. He said he himself had made one too few moves in his career.

After considering several other openings where we checked out the towns, I applied to a position in Rochester, New York, was interviewed and hired. My interview was with the vocal music director for the Rochester City School District. I asked for a syllabus for music in junior high. The director showed me a section on syncopation. I laughed aloud when I saw the example was *Carry Me Back to Old Virginny*.

"Who came up with this rather poor example?" I asked. The director simply replied that he had developed this curriculum himself. After that remark, I was surprised I was still hired. It was said at the interview that being in the same district ten years was a good recommendation. I was hired to teach at Madison High School.

I was so proud of Bill when he received the Distinguished Service Award from the New York State School Music Association.

Friends told us we would not like being in a big city. They predicted we would not like Rochester because it was a big, cold city where no one would know and love us as they did in Delevan. Time was moving fast. The school year was over. We had made no plans for selling our Delevan home or for buying a house in Rochester. We were committed for June and July as assistant director of the St. John's Summer Camp at the foot of Bear Mountain in the Catskills.

As our good fortune continued, we received a letter soon after arriving in camp from Norma Brand in Rochester, New York, who said a friend of a friend informed her that we were moving to Rochester. She enclosed the real estate section of a Rochester paper. She continued to send letters alerting us to the housing market.

Every day in August, we were in Delevan packing, hoping to sell the house and making house-hunting trips when the Urban League of Rochester—through our Realtor, Milton Moss—called to ask us to participate in a study of discrimination in housing patterns. He was the first certified African-American Realtor in Rochester.

Nathalie and John Wilson were early Rochester friends. We were introduced by Milton
Moss, our Realtor and one of the first black Realtors in Rochester. We and the Wilsons
took each other's children on their driving lessons.

Our Realtor, Milton Moss, on the left with artist Calvin Hubbard, made us feel welcome
and at home when we arrived in Rochester. Milton's wife, Vivian, is on the right in the
next photograph with Sue Leone, our backyard neighbor and good friend. My husband,
Bill, worked with Calvin at Madison High School.

Photo by Denise Batiste Photography.

Gene and Joy Ferguson are our perennial Rochester bridge partners. They offered to let us live on their top floor before we found a house. Gene and Bill met in Buffalo, where they were both involved in the United Methodist Church quadrennial Emphasis Committee while we lived in Delevan. Gene was active in Metro Act, a predominantly white ministerial group that supported FIGHT in its demands for community racial equality. Metro Act invited Chicago neighborhood organizer Sol Alinsky to assist in the grass-roots efforts for equal rights for African-Americans after the 1964 race riots. We did not arrive until 1969. Gene shared with us the stories of controversy in his church congregation over his support of the FIGHT organization. We continue to be friends as we solve the world's problems over bridge games on a regular basis.

Theophilus Tyson with Howard Coles, owner and publisher of the African-American newspaper, *Frederick Douglass' Voice*. Howard Coles was the embodiment of Frederick Douglass. He collected books and works of Douglass. He was the Rochester authority on Douglass' life and times. When we first arrived in Rochester, he came to visit us and to invite us to play an active role in the political and social life in Rochester. After that surprise first meeting, we met on a regular basis to discuss political issues and challenges. He supported me when I ran for office.

The study involved Ruth and I and teaming up with a white woman to look for rental housing, since we thought we might have to rent while we looked for a home. Ruth and I answered an advertisement for an apartment rental and, as expected, were usually turned down. The white woman would answer the same ad and, in most cases, would be offered the apartment. I always wore a dress shirt, jacket and tie. Ruth wore a dress or skirt and blouse. The white woman was dressed down in an ill-fitting dress and sometimes flip-flops instead of shoes. Some might say this study was a form of entrapment rather than revelation, but we didn't think so, and neither did the courts. Ruth had a similar experience in finding her first apartment in Cleveland, Ohio, a few years earlier.

Several homes were found through Norma Brand, who had been sending us real-estate ads. She offered her own home as a base for our house-hunting. We accepted her offer. We arrived at her house to find a note on the door telling us where we could find the key. The note said something had come up and she had to leave. She told us there was food in the refrigerator, refreshments in the bar and a comfortable guest room awaited us if we chose to spend the night. What a gracious welcome to Rochester from a woman we had not yet met.

Near the end of August, we still had not found a suitable apartment or home. The Realtor told us he would find temporary housing for us and, on our first day of moving to Rochester, asked us to come to his home for dinner to meet his wife, Vivian, and their family. Fortunately, Ruth called his wife to confirm because she learned that he had not told his wife of our dinner invitation. Vivian became a lifelong friend and we both became portrait-painting students of artist Luvon Sheppard, founder of the Allofus Art Workshop.

Milton informed us that he was unsuccessful in finding us temporary housing, so we could stay with his family. We accepted, expecting to stay a single night, but it turned into several days. I finally said if we did not find something the next day, we would go to the local motel. He did find *something* but it was almost beyond description. The stove was so bad that we used an electric frying pan to prepare our meals. We took the place anyway because by then we had put in a bid on a house on Arvine Heights in the Nineteenth Ward as Norma had suggested. It would be two weeks before we could close. For days, we cleaned our new house—I after working at Madison High School during the day.

Ruth was quite touched one day when a neighbor came down the street with a pot of coffee and two cups to welcome us to the neighborhood. Though Ruth is a tea drinker, she happily drank the coffee and felt welcomed to our new home. Our sense of belonging was sealed by three events: Norma opening her home to us, the Realtor hosting us in his own home and a kindly neighbor bringing coffee to Ruth.

Left to right: Shawnequa with mother June, Crystal, Greg, Bill and I celebrating being a family at 30 Arvine Heights.

Photo by Denise Batiste Photography.

Phyllis Brault remains a friend. We first met through the AAUW (American Association of University Women) interest group "Couples Cooking." It was Phyllis who lent us her home to make those momentous decisions on whether to run for City Council and the State Senate. Our children remained special friends throughout their childhood. She was Greg's first boss when she and her husband owned several apothecary shops. They wanted Greg to attend pharmacy school but, like his mother, Greg preferred to chart his own course.

Photo by Denise Batiste Photography.

When Bill and Sylvia Kamell moved in across the street from us on Arvine Heights in the Nineteenth Ward, we and our children became instant friends. They had three girls and a boy who fit in between our children in ages. The children ran back and forth between the houses, having lunch and sometimes dinner at whichever house they happened to be at mealtime. Bill Kamell was doing his internship in orthopedic surgery at the University of Rochester Strong Hospital and Sylvia was a midwife. When their daughter Sonya was born, father Kamell was off at a medical conference in California. We as the backup hospital ride, took Sylvia to the hospital to deliver baby Sonya Ruth. Sylvia still laughs about the expression on my Bill's face when he had to come to tell Sylvia that her Bill had checked out of the hotel and could not be reached. She thought that was very funny and immediately gave my husband Bill her brother-in-law's name and telephone number. My Bill was able to reach him to let him know his new daughter had arrived early. Left to right: Sylvia Kamell, Sonia Ruth Kamell, our daughter Crystal, Lisa Kamell, and my high school and college debate partner Joe Munk.

Mom Scott and Bill's Aunt Ethel, Gregory and June. Our daughter Crystal, who was born well after this photograph was taken, has grown to look much like Mom Scott. We are standing in the front yard of the house that was built by hand by Bill's maternal grandfather, James E. Dunn.

Bill's grandfather James E. Dunn, who built the three-story house at 13 Minerva Place with his own hands in White Plains, New York. He was also a master gardener.

Back row left to right: Rodney, Bill, Bob. Front row: June, Dad, Mother and me.

Brother Rodney's Death

The effect of Rodney's death on various members of the family and Rodney's fiancée was a profound one. Thirty seven years later, my sisters, brothers and LuRachelle (his fiancée) speak of their sadness as if it happened yesterday. I remember my own reaction to the diagnoses of lung cancer. The phone call is as clear in my mind as yesterday. Bill and I were visiting with Mom and Dad Scott. It was a bright August day at the end of our camp St. John's work for the summer of 1971.

The shades were drawn to keep out the sun in this rectangle-shaped room with its four chairs, a television set, a beautiful set of golden brocade draperies on the front window and lace curtains on the side window. Mom Scott was out shopping. I was half dozing, lulled by the muffled sounds of Dad Scott and Bill laughing. I was thinking about how blessed and peaceful my life was with a great extended family to embrace me, adventures in our new Nineteenth Ward neighborhood in Rochester and no apparent crisis on the horizon. The children, Greg and June, had been put down for their afternoon naps in an upstairs bedroom in this house that Grandpa Dunn built with his own hands.

Rodney had left our house in Rochester to travel back to Michigan to see his childhood doctor about not feeling well. He was a legal intern in the Public Defender's Office in Rochester. The ringing of the phone seemed exceptionally loud as it jarred me out of pleasant half-dreams. Bill answered the phone and somehow before I took the phone, I knew it was not good news. Mom said to me, "Rodney has been diagnosed with lung cancer." Mom later told me that she knew it was a serious, possibly terminal sickness, when he got off the plane in Detroit, the nearest commercial airport to Albion, ninety-eight miles due northwest. I remember saying, "Oh no," handing the phone back to my husband and dissolving into sobs on the couch. I heard Bill say we would be there as soon as possible. Those tears flowed for Rodney and his fiancée.

Somewhere in my mind, I remember Aunt Ruth's advice, "If something hurts really badly, it is all right to cry." So I gave way to my deepest sorrow in all my thirty-one years. My body-racking crying must have lasted for a long time, as I heard Dad Scott say, "Do you think we should call the doctor?" My tears then began to subside as my husband tried to comfort me. The next few days were a blur as we prepared to leave our

White Plains vacation early and drive to Michigan.

Upon arriving in Michigan, we dropped off our suitcases and left the children with sitters at the 619 Center Street house and drove to the hospital, where surgery was to be performed in Battle Creek nineteen miles away.

Mom, Dad, June, Bob and Bill greeted us with almost a group hug, silently praying for the best outcome of the surgery. I remember Dad's shoulders sagging as if he bore a load too heavy to carry and Mom's eyes filled with a peaceful, yet prayerful resolution. It seems as though we sat in silence for a long time. Through the next several hours, there were reminiscences of fun with Rodney and some attempt to be hopeful about law school graduation next year, when we all planned to gather and celebrate. We set aside our private fears and waited with trepidation when the nurse arrived to say the doctor had finished surgery. Rod was stable and the doctor would talk to us shortly. There was a collective sigh of relief tinged with some fear of the consultation to follow. The tall, pale doctor with dark hair and penetrating dark eyes walked into the private waiting room. We held our collective breath almost spellbound as he sighed and said, "I did the best I could." He shook his head and said, "I had to take the whole lung. It looks very bad. All I can tell you is that you ought to pray, because I couldn't do …" Tears started to stream down the doctor's face. "He's too young to die. He was a smoker, you know." At which point, Dad broke the spell with an expletive. "Smoking couldn't be it! I am a three-pack-a-day man and I have only one lung!" Dad did not literally pound the walls, but his words did.

Over the next few hours, days, all time stood still. We called Rodney's fiancée who was out on the West Coast with family, and met her at the Detroit Airport. We had Rodney moved to the local hospital, and spent shifts of family members, friends and LuRachelle around Rod's bed at Albion Memorial Hospital day and night. Rodney asked Mother to buy him a crucifix, which he wore to his grave. None of the other family members shared their private times with him to any great degree. It was as though we were all connected through Rod's pain and suffering, but also thereby isolated from each other. I now know that lots of things went on behind the scenes, but my focus was on Rodney and what might I say to him to soothe the obvious pain he was suffering. We had several conversations. I only remember Rodney saying, "I love you guys. I love Lu." In what now seems to me to be more concern for me than for him, he asked me to pray. I kneeled, trying to remember soothing words. All I could think of to say (as many times as I have prayed, day and sometimes all night when I felt troubled) was the Lord's Prayer. Then he said, "Thank you." At that point, Rodney called out, "Mom!" I hurried to get her. She came into the room and said, "Honey, I'm here," and he breathed his last breath. I am told that he and my brothers played cards one night. Mom was in and out of the room most of the time. I don't remember Dad coming to the hospital. It was years later that, according to Lu, I learned my siblings took her aside to say, "You have to be strong for my mom and dad." So when my Mom told her she needed to stay home and rest, she missed that last day of Rodney's life. She felt she could not show the bereft and abandoned emotions she felt thinking of all the wonderful life plans they had made together that had been cut short for no reason.

Since Lu and I both lived in Rochester, New York, we formed a natural bond. We spent many days with her curled up in my living room rocking chair just being sad and my uttering what I hoped were encouraging remarks. She was a teacher in the Rochester City School District, recruited by the late Alean Rush, who organized Project Unique, designed to find promising young African-American students enrolled in southern schools to come to Rochester to teach in the Rochester School District. They were promised that the district would pay for their master's degree work. A number of the first and present African-American leadership in the Central Office and in the schools came from that program.

Our friendship grew over the years and remains strong. We may not talk on the phone for six months, then pick up a conversation as though it was yesterday. I knew by her reputation that she was an excellent teacher and would have made a great Rochester City School District leader. However, Rochester became too sad a place for her and she moved to Seattle, where she married a very controlling and abusive man, had two beautiful girls and taught for some time at the University of Washington. She eventually established her own consulting business and was married again to a more loving and sharing husband, Michael Atkins.

The distance did not seem to weaken our relationship any more than our six-month breaks between phone conversations. Over the years, she and I have shared religious challenges, child raising strategies, business ventures and membership in Leadership America. Bill and I had asked her to be godmother to our youngest daughter, Crystal, who was born the year after Rodney died—the year he would have graduated. At five years old,

Crystal became Lu's flower girl for her wedding. We have maintained our close relationship over the years and Lu still shares with me her feelings of regret that she and Rod did not run away and get married as Rodney had pressed that summer before he discovered the lung cancer. Lu felt reluctant to marry without her grandmother's blessing, because she promised before leaving for college that she would not marry without it. Lu told me recently that during those early years after Rodney's death, she only could relieve the weight of her sorrow by uncontrollable crying, the desire of which overcame her occasionally.

If I had known that then, I would have told her—after a decent time had passed—about one of my Aunt Ruth's stories. I observed one day to Aunt Ruth, "Every now and then you seem very sad." She sighed deeply and said, "It is because we were never allowed to cry about my brother's death." After what must have been my quizzical look, she continued. "When our oldest brother was in high school, he died in a football game after receiving a head injury. My father said, 'I don't want any of you to cry. This is God's will.'" I can still see her shaking her head with the braids wrapped around her head like a crown and saying, "If you ever have something that hurts that badly, you just have to let it out. Cry regardless of what others observing might say." Her brother must have died in the late 1920s. The family was the only black family farming in Saline, Michigan, about five country miles from Albion. Her parents had strict rules about not letting "white people" see members of the family crying, fearful or sweating because it would make them appear vulnerable.

This was a common constraint—the "color line"—taught in those days by many Negroes to their children, presumably to keep them from being too visible to whites who may be inclined to notice and bully them if they saw vulnerability. Unfortunately, some blacks still hold such fears in the 21st century. Such feelings often weigh heavily on the minds of black people, blocking creativity, confidence and accomplishments. This fear and lack of trust of the white society is especially deeply ingrained in African-Americans who grew up in the south. Under slavery, it was a crime, sometimes punishable by death, to teach a Negro to read or write. Historically speaking, slavery did not end so long ago and the rush of post-Reconstruction era "Jim Crow" laws assured many states that the former slave would not grow beyond the "color line" established by the white community. Even in the 1950s, adults and children were expected to move off of sidewalks whenever a white person approached them, bow their heads, avoid direct eye contact and feign ignorance in acknowledgment of the superior status of whites. It is no wonder that the residual effects of mental slavery still exist in some parts of society in the 21st century. Current experiences that are reminiscent of the old segregation and Jim Crow laws bring some African-Americans today to say, "Now do you *really* believe you can trust white people?" All Americans, regardless of color or ethnicity, must be aware of this history—to challenge the old ways and to work hard to make equal opportunities.

Not a day goes by that I don't think of Rodney. Everyone in our family sought to mourn Rodney's loss and heal in a different way. I think my mother accepted his death quietly as if she could do nothing but accept God's will even after losing her first son, Gilbert. Dad never did accept Rodney's death, and it leaves a big void in Lu's and my hearts.

I ran across a letter my brother wrote to me in his senior year of high school saying he had decided not to go to college because he wanted to make his own way in life. He also said he knew that the family would not like his decision but he hoped we would understand and accept his decision to manage his own life.

The next thing I knew, the high school football coach set up an appointment for Rod at Olivet College in Olivet, Michigan, and he was enrolled as a freshman. That spring, Martin Luther King, Jr., was assassinated in Memphis, Tennessee, and Rodney was selected to represent his fraternity at the funeral. Rod was so moved by the challenges that faced America in 1968 and the civil rights cause that MLK stood for that he determined then that he knew what he wanted to do with his life.

Dad was so ecstatic to hear that Rod was pursuing a law degree, his own desired goal, that he was lifted out of his own depression for a few years. Rod went to a summer pre-law program at Akron University, then to Howard, where he would have graduated in the class of 1971.

We may never understand why such a promising life was cut short, but I can tell you that Rod's life was not without influence on everyone he touched.

Cousin Hattie Madison and her husband in the garden of their apartment complex in Chicago. She owned a number of apartments and was wealthy by our family's standards. I spent many summer vacations there. She offered to pay for my education if I would attend college to be an attorney. She wanted to adopt one of us Holland children as her own child, as she had no children of her own. Mom and Dad, of course, declined. Cousin Hattie sent us boxes of clothes and often attended special family events, including my wedding.

It was Hattie's cousin UV, at her apartment in New York City, whom I visited the year I met Bill. I went to New York City myself after teaching for a year. Four of us classmates, including Sally and Kay, were to share our teaching adventures. Bill's brother gave me a few names to look up but I took Bill's father's advice and did not. I called Hattie's cousin UV, and she was very excited to hear from me and wanted me to visit her. Then I heard the caution in her voice. "I can't let you come when my husband or anyone is around because no one knows I am colored. She asked me to visit during the day when her husband was away at work, because he was white and she was black. Today this seems strange, but in the days of segregation and discrimination, these cautions were firmly in place. Intermarriage between the races was silent because it could destroy a marriage or threaten her life. I arrived when her husband and maid were gone. She asked about family with concern and caring. She asked me about my life and I felt that family connection, but I also felt the distance she kept because she necessarily kept me away from meeting her husband. I did not yet understand the fears and controls that segregation and discrimination keep in the lives of African-Americans, denying their own siblings and parents. She offered that I visit her again, but I never did. Maybe I was just too busy, but I also felt somewhat angry about her false life. I did not then understand fully the position she must have been in, but now that I am more mature, I have more understanding for the "color line." She lived in the "Jim Crow" years. There were more lynchings and backlashes in the early 1900s than at any other time in our country's history.

Rumors of Jim Crow's Death
Are Greatly Exaggerated

Young people I speak to today have no idea of the discrimination we experienced in our lifetime. They think of segregation and discrimination as a part of our history. Of course, it was we who worked so hard to eradicate it wherever we found it and shield them from the reality.

Overall, I think we have made major strides toward eliminating unjust exclusions of groups of people in our society. I do think there is still a strong undercurrent or backlash against equal rights and opportunity expressed in the new repressive laws that cannot stand the test of time and democracy. It is a last hurrah of fear, ignorance and exclusivity.

One of the most memorable experiences I had with discrimination happened when I was only a second-grader. Sometimes people today, both black and white, struggle to understand the boundaries that limited black Americans when I was a child. The "color lines," as they were called, were invisible, but we learned where they were very young. The boundaries were different in other parts of the country, which presented a challenge to African-Americans who were migrating north from the South or moving to other states for job opportunities.

I grew up in a family environment that encouraged education. I had no idea that there were people in the world who did not share this philosophy for African-Americans.

Both of my parents taught us that we should not be bound by other peoples' prejudices because what we build inside of ourselves—our knowledge and confidence—cannot be taken from us. They taught me the names of products on the grocery store shelves at such an early age that I went to kindergarten knowing more words than the average child entering school.

My parents surrounded us with reading material at home so my desire to learn to read seemed natural. Dad collected books and periodicals. He subscribed to the *Chicago Defender, Detroit Free Press,* the *Battle Creek Enquirer, Newsweek, Time* magazine, *Life* magazine and *Readers' Digest.* He read even more broadly by trading magazines with one of the Albion's early teachers, Ruth Ferguson. Our family was so close to her that I called her Aunt Ruth.

I remember my dad reading the Sunday paper and commenting on world events, mumbling his disapproval or cheering his approval of articles he read. He and Mom had extensive conversations about what they were reading even though they read sometimes strikingly different books. I learned music and other things from Aunt Ruth when, at the age of six, I cleaned house with her for five cents an hour.

Aunt Ruth lived in what we called the gingerbread house across Center Street on the corner of Albion Street. Her house was a small, asphalt brick-covered immaculate home. On Saturday afternoons, Mother allowed me to visit Aunt Ruth. She taught me how to shine floors, china and silverware. Her house outclassed any I knew anywhere. After work, we took a break. We sat in the kitchen filled with the sweet aroma of baked chicken, pound cake and peach cobbler. The sounds of Marian Anderson and Paul Robeson carried in from the victrola in the small library at the front of the house. Dad borrowed many books from her extensive home library ... and I learned to value both books and music.

That love of books carried through the generations to my own children. Both Bill and I have surrounded ourselves with books. We read to our children on road trips, instilling in them the love of books.

The world was opened to me by these books and periodicals and by the encouragement of those around me in my home. Not every family is so fortunate ... and some are even publicly *discouraged* as when I was a second-grader. The city library sponsored a summer reading contest in which I wanted to participate. The librarian informed me, without reservation, that Negro children were not allowed to take books out of the library.

"Well," I asked, "Can I read in the library?"

"Sure," she said with a shrug that suggested that it would be futile. That was more years ago than I care to remember, but I have not forgotten that attitude nor the sting that it carried. But I was not to be deterred—and maybe it even strengthened me.

While the reading contest was under way at the library, I read voraciously and watched with excitement as the multi-colored slips of paper with my name on them were pasted in the library window with each book I completed. The librarian was skeptical. She questioned me intensely about each book to be sure I wasn't cheating.

I read a book from every section in the library. I chose one on spiritualism which coincidentally, began in Rochester, New York. That deep subject really raised the eyebrows of the skeptical librarian.

I won a book of my choice in that contest.

Maybe that experience reading so many books in a short space of time served me well in another way. I began to master speed reading. In high school and college, I could speed through both affirmative and negative arguments. I could challenge my debate opponent, knowing the entire text of his or her material. My ninth-grade debate coach, Ethel Fleenor, wrote in my report card: "Ruth has a plethora of studied material and quotations at her fingertips which she uses extremely well in her debates to confound her opponents." I must admit, I didn't fully know what she meant then, but her training laid the foundation for Peggy Taylor and me to win the Michigan Statewide Debate Contest in 1956 and with Joe Munk at Albion College over the Oxford, England, team in 1957.

Another memorable experience with discrimination took place when I was very young.

I loved Austin Elementary School, which I attended from kindergarten through fifth grade. I still remember my kindergarten teacher, Mrs. Johnson, and first-grade teacher, Mrs. Ullery. They told wonderful stories and acted them out as they read. Sometimes we were assigned stories to act out.

In one public presentation, we were assigned parts. I wanted to be the princess. My teacher said, "But princesses have long golden hair and fair skin."

That stereotype slowed me down some, but not much. She then assigned me to be a frog. My mother asked what kind of a dress I needed to wear and I replied "yellow." Of course yellow was to be worn by the ducks.

When the play was performed, I was the only frog in a yellow dress croaking, "Galump."

The teacher did not remove me from the play and said nothing to me. I am not sure anyone in the audience even noticed my silent protest. My mother, of course, noticed that I was seated with the frogs, but was dressed like the ducks. My mother assured me that it was fine for me to play any role I wanted, but that once I accepted a role, I should have played it. I should have been the best frog that I could be. "If you can't be the moon, be the star, and be the best of whatever you are."

But then we moved across the railroad tracks from Ann Street to Eaton Street and then to Center Street. It was, according to the Albion School District, required that I attend sixth grade at West Ward School. We later learned that was not true. All the white children went to Dalrymple School on that side of town.

I was a little afraid to be going to West Ward School because we were often threatened by teachers at the Austin Elementary School with, "If you don't behave, I will send you to West Ward." But I gathered my courage and, with Dad's attitude, went off to "slay the dragon" at the new school.

It didn't take long for me to understand what the Austin Elementary teachers meant when they contrasted West Ward with their school. West Ward was remarkably inferior to the other elementary schools. West Ward was four rooms with no hallways, only closets to separate the rooms. Students had to pass through the front two rooms to reach the other two. The first two rooms in front were kindergarten through second grades, while the back rooms were third and fourth grades in one room and fifth and sixth in the second. There was a basement with a concrete slab floor and brick walls. Mrs. Biggs, one of the two Michigan-certified teachers, taught kindergarten through second; Mrs. Stewart taught third grade; Mrs. Ferguson, the other Michigan-certified teacher and intellectual friend of my dad's, taught fifth grade; and Mrs. Holmes taught sixth.

Teachers tried to make the best of the limited resources. Mrs. Ferguson provided art and music. Mrs. Biggs believed that sixth-graders should know something about art, so she and Mrs. Ferguson sponsored an art/music contest for which each student would write a paper and draw a picture about a famous musician. As an honor, the picture would later be painted on the school's basement wall. My picture of Marian Anderson was chosen. With pride, I enlarged the portrait and painted it on the wall of the school. This exercise led to a lifelong appreciation of art.

My sister June and brother Bob also attended West Ward Elementary School. They have their own stories. Bob's one strong memory is of fourth grade, when pleurisy kept him on bed rest most of the year. Mom arranged for him to have his lessons taught to him at home. Bob honed his imagination, like Dad, as he passed the hours in bed, his world existing in what he saw pass by the bedroom window. However, he was not anxious to return to West Ward.

The condition of West Ward was poor enough, but the books were old, often missing covers and some pages. From 1945, before any of his children attended West Ward, Dad tried for a number of years—a full decade before the famous Brown vs. the Board of Education—to get the Albion, Michigan, City Fathers to improve the one segregated school, but he failed to garner their support. In fact, they never even recorded his remarks in the minutes when he spoke before them. At some point, Dad started a chapter of the NAACP and spoke to the City Fathers as the organization's official spokesperson.

Over a number of months, he put up fact sheets on light poles around the town, announcing the age of the text books, the placement of the West Ward graduates into non-college-bound courses because of their low test scores, select incidents of corporal punishment at the segregated school, and the lack of certification of the principal and one teacher. No one knew where this information was coming from and it baffled the City Fathers. Dad carefully researched his facts, anticipating a challenge from the City Fathers and a baffled, uninformed white community. Conversations in the black community turned into an incensed uproar as they picketed the joint city council and school board.

At a public meeting in 1953, people asked, "What can we do about this school?"

Dad said, "You could keep your children home."

This, I think, is when the relationship between Dad and teacher Ruth Ferguson cooled for a while. Was she concerned that she would lose her job? Was she concerned for the children's education or safety? I don't know.

A carry-over from an earlier century, whites held all the political power. Many communities in the thirty years following World War I had little understanding of or familiarity with the black citizens living there. So many white people during these days lived in their own world, preoccupied with their own economic struggles and with little contact with people of color. My dad's decision to confront the City Fathers with the inequities that segregation brought enlightened the white community at large.

Holland Park was dedicated in the early 1970s on the site of the old West Ward Elementary School in the southwest part of Albion, Michigan, in honor of Dad's work to close that substandard school. I presented my painting of him to Albion Hospital, where Dad served on the board of directors. It hung in the board room for two decades before the hospital was demolished and the painting was returned to me.

The summer of 1953, a year after Dad's boycott, the U.S. Supreme Court ruled in Brown vs. The Board of Education that "separate is not equal." For years before the boycott, discussions among black parents took place in black churches in Albion. Dad laid out the facts to black parents who were becoming increasingly angry. The parents determined to make one more presentation to the City Fathers, demanding that they make major changes at West Ward or close it. If the officials would not listen, there would be a boycott of classes the first week of school.

The officials felt the pressure enough to ask my mother to convince Dad to withdraw his pressure and they would transfer their children to another school. Mom's reply was, "Even if I could convince Bob, who has his own mind, I would not because he is right." She added, "Furthermore, I don't want any special favors for my children. You need to do what is right for all children."

The boycott worked. West Ward was closed in 1953 and the black students were integrated throughout the District. The building was demolished. A park sprang up in its place. In the early 1970s when my father died, the park was renamed Holland Park. The inscription on the park sign reads, "This park is dedicated to Robert Holland who fought the building of the West Ward School, so that we might be free to fight the 'West Wards' of the mind."

While Dad was fighting for equality and justice, my friend Vern Kinsey and I did what many people of color do—we made the best of the conditions we lived with. All of us as students realized that a pitifully limited amount of learning took place, except in Mrs. Ferguson's special "unofficial" classes in art and music. For reasons that escape me, Mrs. Holmes was named principal. Some of the more disruptive boys used to lift the wig off of her head with the crooked edge of the window pole as she nodded off to sleep in front of the class. The laughter of the class would awaken her and the startled Mrs. Holmes would declare a recess. The students would file out of the classroom for recess while Vern and I stayed behind making the best of this bad situation at West Ward because "We don't want to be behind when we go to high school and college." We decided to teach each other. We assigned reading books, lessons and tests for each other daily. We allowed recess only when our assigned work was completed. As a bonus for good work, we plotted to take trips together to Paris and Africa. We knew we would be tested in early junior high to place us on a college track based on our exam scores. We were determined to do well.

We never went together to those idyllic places, but we are still friends to this day. After graduating from college suma cum laude, Vern became a journalist. She married and learned, following her marriage, that her African husband was a prince who did not reveal his status until they actually went to meet his family. The family, needless to say, was not pleased that he had married this "American girl" who obviously did not understand that her role as his wife was to deliver him fine, strong sons and to manage the lesser wives, which he fortunately did not yet have.

Vern's husband convinced his parents to wait a while before demanding this status symbol from their son. A year later, luckily, a son was born to Vern and her "prince." At night, Vern could have her son sleep beside her. However, she had a growing uneasiness with her husband's family as her child was taken away from her breast to be fed, watched and taught by a nurse of the family's choice. This filled her with a growing dread—"What had she gotten herself into?" Vern began to formulate a plan to deal with this less-than-desirable situation much as she and I had in our earlier years dealt with inadequate teaching.

With the help of a sympathetic household servant, Vern and her infant son escaped to the nearest large city, where she flew back to her family in Michigan. She promptly filed for divorce. The pain Vern suffered during her marriage to a man she did not fully know unfolded over the years. Vern's response to me about her time in Africa was cryptically, "When it gets dark in Africa, it gets really dark."

Vern went on to law school, became assistant Michigan State Attorney General and later married a widowed OB/GYN specialist, helped him raise his two sons along with her African son, and gave birth to fourth son. They have lived for years in Toledo, Ohio, where we could visit them on our trips back to Michigan. She and her mother were like a second family to me. My children—Crystal, June and Greg—visited Vern when they went to visit their grandparents in Albion, Michigan, in the summer. Vern and I share a bond that allowed us to pick up a conversation after years apart and never miss a word.

That's what became of some of the young African-Americans who attended segregated schools. They made the best of their educational opportunities and, through great effort, lived productive, useful lives. Today, discrimination takes many different forms, making it difficult to pinpoint just what is discriminatory. Often, what sparks the public discussion of race is not discriminatory at all, but reveals an undercurrent—a less visible, discriminatory, public opinion. While we have made major strides in integration, education and job opportunities, African-Americans still experience resistance to full acceptance—they are often stereotyped to certain jobs, lifestyles and places in our society. Blog discussions reflect an unsettled balance between the races, a recognition of the need for a paradigm shift and how to achieve this. Part of this shift requires an acknowledgment of realities: "We are all different. We are all alike."

When Bill and I first came to Rochester, we were asked to speak to groups that indicated that African-Americans in the city were tired of talking about race. Bill sometimes told his students who talked about living in the ghetto that they didn't know what a ghetto was until they saw those

From the journey of our career planning at West Ward School Judge Vernelis Kinsey Armstrong in her office in the Akron, Ohio, Court Building.

in New York City. In other words, our experiences are relative. When we listen to people from other countries today speaking about the genocide, racial and ethnic cleansing and political civil war, it gives American racial relations a different perspective—a more global understanding that African-Americans do not alone face challenges. African-Americans have made great strides and will continue to do so, but the weight of our slave history must be cast off while we embrace and imitate the accomplishments of actual leaders like Frederick Douglass and the more modern Martin Luther King, Jr., who worked to "overcome" Jim Crow.

Not all discrimination is racial or even intended. In the 1970s, for example, our political, cultural and social practices were changing, and the women's rights movement was growing stronger. Most of the U.S. business leaders before the 1970s were men, and while women were entering business, they were not readily admitted into the arenas in which men made their business deals. The struggles were usually fought by individuals rather than by group demonstrations. For example, I challenged the men-only Garden Café outside of McCurdy's department store inside Rochester's Midtown Mall. I can understand that when Rosa Parks said she was tired and just wanted to sit down on the bus in 1955, she wasn't planning to start a bus boycott.

I was simply hungry one day when I was at Midtown Mall, and I needed to eat lunch before going to lead my next City Council committee meeting. I took a menu and a seat, and after a few minutes, I realized no waiters had come to my table. I looked around and saw that there were only men seated at the tables; however, I shrugged my shoulders and remained seated. After about ten minutes, the manager of the café, who knew me from the Nineteenth Ward Community Association, came out and whispered to me, "Ruth, why are you doing this?"

I, of course, said, "What?"

"We don't serve women. It's not my policy. It's the policy of the owners."

I replied, "But I need something to eat."

He replied. "I will serve you this time, but please don't do it again."

Suddenly, after that day, more and more women went to eat at that café. There were no signs forbidding women from eating there, but you definitely got that unwelcome feeling when you overstepped the limits as a woman. Women protested in their own quiet way that being barred from men-only clubs and meeting rooms, as well as golf clubs, hampered or prevented them from making the same lucrative business deals or network the way men did. Some organizations changed; others did not. Several private clubs in Rochester extended invitations to me to become a member, but I "gracefully" declined. I did not like the "exclusive" character of these clubs. Other private clubs were also challenged in the 1970s. It was during this time, when American culture was changing and questioning the old barriers, that I experienced workplace discrimination.

There were few women officers in banks in Rochester and around the country. So the offer from the president, Al Hook, to become an officer at Community Savings Bank was exciting to me. I was hired as a special assistant to the president to discuss and plan new products and bank strategies for remaining competitive. One of my assignments was special research projects regarding state and federal laws, including the Community Reinvestment Act. I was appointed Community Reinvestment Officer and Corporate Secretary.

I became the sole director of the bank's charitable trust, which allowed me to make many decisions on community grants. Additional responsibilities included designing training for tellers and community relations, as well as the bank's designee to the YMCA board.

I worked at the bank for thirteen years. The leadership was supportive of my working as an officer, but the male officers showed and expressed their professional jealousy and objection to me as a woman. My desk was eventually moved out of the executive suite near the bank's president and to the middle of construction.

The president retired. The new administration seemed to have difficulty helping me plan my future in the bank. They assigned me to be a branch manager at the Times Square office at Exchange and State Streets in downtown Rochester. It was hinted to me that all the senior management in the bank had been managers at the Times Square office. Marian Johnson was my capable, supportive backup assistant manager. That adventure led to becoming a regional branch manager with eight branches under me. After a couple years of as a branch regional manager, I sat down to discuss my career path with management.

In the meantime, the bank merged with Rochester Savings Bank to become Rochester Community Savings Bank. It was suggested that if I had an MBA, the bank could understand where to place me without complaints from other mostly white, male department heads.

My first response was, "I have the equivalent of two masters' degrees. Why do I need an MBA? I rethought my position and proposed to be sent to the Harvard Business School for senior management development. The retort was "What if you can't pass the classes?"

My answer was, "I have never seen a course I couldn't pass, let alone ace."

Through several negotiating sessions, the bank agreed to fund the first year of operation for my new business. However, one sticking point was that the bank requested that our agreement include that any new successful product or process would belong to the bank. My response was, "I'll be happy to give you credit, but products and process will belong to Scott Associates, Inc." One of the national banking newsletters, *The Bottom Line*, that year touted me as the most interesting new business idea of the year! That was 1989, when I left City Council and the bank to launch my own business as a consultant to banks about community reinvestment.

My husband, Bill, experienced discrimination, as well. He and I often share our stories of the discrimination we faced growing up in our respective communities in Albion, Michigan, and in White Plains, New York, a bustling bedroom community only a short train ride from Grand Central Station in New York City. We both were undaunted and refused to be held by slights, discrimination or outright restrictions of minorities. Despite his high school guidance counselor not calling him to the office for interviews, Bill made his own appointments. Bill called the hotel where the interviewer was staying and he wound up being interviewed in the car ride to the hotel and was accepted as a music major at SUNY Fredonia. In some ways, Bill lived a rather sheltered life in White Plains, but his father knew what his son could experience when he left the safety of home in the North. My folks never allowed the Holland children to travel when Mother went south to Florida to visit. It appears Bill's father had similar feelings about the South. I'll let Bill tell you his story.

My brother's best friend and my dad's candidate for successful attorney Jesse Womach, Albion College President Peter T. Mitchell, a special friend and Aunt Ruth's niece Nancy Woods Whitfield, me, my husband Bill and my brother Bill.

America, the Land of the Free

—Bill's Story

I always loved music. I completed two years at Fredonia before I joined the U.S. Army and auditioned for the West Point Special Band. I had some contacts that helped me get into the regular Army Band School at Fort Knox, Kentucky. After taking eight weeks of basic training at Fort Dix in New Jersey, I received the assignment to Fort Knox. My father was visibly shaken to hear that I would be in the South. A few months earlier, Emmett Till, a young black man from Chicago who was accused of *looking* at a white girl, was lynched in Mississippi. I soon learned the realities of life for African-Americans in other parts of the United States—in uniform or not. A "colored" man had his "place" in the South and many parts of the North.

A private company operated the railroad station on the military base at Fort Knox. When I ran into one of my friends from Fredonia, I was asked to go to the train station with him to purchase a ticket for his fiancée to come for a visit. There for the first time I saw "white only" and "colored" signs at the drinking fountains.

The next eight weeks of training at Band School at Fort Knox were uneventful. I was reassigned to Fort Leonard Wood in Missouri. Four men were assigned to travel together from Fort Knox to Fort Leonard Wood.

We left Fort Knox for Louisville, where we were to catch a bus to Fort Leonard Wood. At the station in St. Louis, Missouri, I saw the sign "colored waiting room" but made the decision to wait with the three white soldiers as military protocol dictated. Soon after I sat down, a Negro porter, as they were referred to, came to me and said I could not sit there. I told him the circumstances, but the porter insisted. He suggested I move to the "colored" waiting room. The white station manager came and profanely ordered me to move or he would call the police. I told him that military orders directed we stay together. I told him that civilian police had no authority over me if military police were on the premises. He went to get the military police but turned a deep shade of red when he saw they were both Negroes. The manager returned to his office and nothing more was said.

Women of Strength Form Circles of Power

Women Who Inspired and Strengthened Me

As a student at Albion College, I used to burn the midnight oil in Dean Hall, talking to my friends, fantasizing about our futures and exchanging ideas. One of my fantasies was to travel around the world and sit at the feet of the famous philosophers to glean their knowledge about life and the world. Throughout my lifetime, I have been blessed with meeting and having fellowship with so many wonderful people. The women I describe seem to me to be the philosophers at whose feet I once longed to sit. God in his wisdom had granted me that gift. There were also men, but these women were representative of so many of my encounters, especially fulfilling my need to seek and be surrounded by wisdom.

The following are people who have had a lasting formative influence on who I am today.

Because of the strong legacy of multicultural women and men of faith, whole generations who might have lost their courage and their civilization have, through others' struggles and their tears, found hope in the present and faith in the future. Neither age nor previous condition of servitude diminishes the light of these lives even when they moved from our moment in time to eternity.

Coretta Scott King

Coretta Scott King remains one of the inspirations in my life. It was my good fortune to be drawn into her circle. Her life's work pointed out to black women that they faced two challenges on social and political fronts. Not only were they working to throw off the historical chains that prevented them from reaching their full potential in education and employment as African-Americans, they also had to throw off the shackles that bound them to outdated roles as women. Black men as well as white, American as well as other nationalities and cultures, often held and hold women in a subordinate position socially and politically. Breaking these feminine boundaries followed on the heels of the black civil rights movement.

Following the assassination of Martin Luther King, Jr., in 1968, his wife, Coretta, carried on his vision to end segregation and seek peace and equality. I soon had the opportunity to work with her to achieve this vision.

I was newly appointed to the Rochester City Council in 1977 when Jessie Rattley, vice president of the National League of Cities, invited me to join the league's caucus for Women in Municipal Government (WIMG), of which she was a founding member. She believed there were not enough women elected to municipal positions. She believed, as I do, that women could accomplish great things in their communities on a national level. "Woman's place is in the House and the Senate *and* the Presidency," she said

Jesse invited me to join in her meetings with national leaders as they formulated strategies for the WIMG. This was a great training ground for me as a young, inspired government leader. I so clearly remember the day Jesse invited me to her suite in the Washington, D.C., Hilton during the National League of Cities Annual Conference. I was excited as I met this modest woman named Coretta Scott King. I was swept into her cause as she spoke of the need for elected women (and men) to press Congress and the House to set aside the birthday of Martin Luther King, Jr., as a national holiday to keep alive his vision to end discrimination. For the next fifteen years, Coretta pushed Congress, assemblies, governors and presidents. She was responsible for six million petitions being presented to Congress. She enlisted black and white women to join in her quest.

I was taken by her perseverance, but she also showed her human side. In the early 1980s, I was visiting with her in her hotel room to welcome her to Rochester when she confided in me that she was not sure if all her work might be in vain. She was publicly criticized by men close to her husband's circle charging that as a woman she should not be taking away political power that rightly belonged to them. From men and women, she was criticized for leaving her children for lengthy periods of time. I asked her, "Do you still feel called to this purpose of establishing a national holiday?"

She answered yes. To which I replied, "Then you have to go on."

Living in Rochester, I knew of a black man who had achieved an international reputation, led worldwide civil rights movements, spoken words that even after more than a century carry great weight and relevance in our political and social world, is hardly remembered by people outside of Rochester. That man, Frederick Douglass, has only recently been recognized for his great accomplishments and his continued inspiration to us as we continue our march toward freedom.

In Rochester, I was also introduced to the work of Susan B. Anthony, who lived in Rochester and Harriet Tubman, who lived in nearby Auburn, as they worked for women's freedom and the right of women to vote. It was this newly awakened awareness of civil rights that compelled me to join in Coretta's cause.

Finally, in 1983, Martin Luther King, Jr.'s, birthday became a national holiday and is celebrated in many other parts of the world, as well. Subsequently, I was appointed by Mayor Thomas Ryan to form a Rochester committee to establish links between the Martin Luther King, Jr,. State Commission and the Martin Luther King, Jr., Center and Institute for Nonviolence in Atlanta, Georgia. The national center provided educational programs and supporting materials for annual celebrations for commission members in cities throughout the country.

The newly established center worked to develop ways to teach the principles MLK envisioned and to keep the focus on community building. At times, it seemed the focus migrated to ethnic rather than communitywide needs and concerns. For a few years, the center struggled with whether the federal government or the family controlled the legacy. Coretta talked about these preoccupations with divisions instead of the celebration of humanity's unity. She added that the commissions, along with the center, would breathe new life into communitywide activities and celebrations.

In several of my meetings with Coretta, we spoke about raising our children in a public arena. As locally elected public officials, Jesse and I shared our belief with Coretta that our children would inherit the future and that we each had a responsibility to build a firm foundation for and under them in spite of our public commitments. Jessie's daughter went on to become a noted attorney in Newport News, Virginia, while Coretta's children have worked to secure the center and foundation. My children have remained passionately interested in solving community problems. Jesse and I served our respective communities and worked with some national groups. Coretta's reach was worldwide.

The last meeting I had with Coretta was a fleeting one at Ebenezer Baptist Church one Sunday in 1996. Bill and I visited the King center and attended the church service. I did not then realize it would be my last meeting with her. I did take that opportunity to tell her how much I appreciated the opportunity to work with her and to see the fruit of our labor bloom in the Center. I thanked her for not giving up the fight over those long years. In her usual graciousness, she smiled and said, "Thank you. Bless you." And in an unusual gesture of our experience together, she gave me a hug.

Grandma Collins

Me with Grandma Collins.

Grandma Collins is known by many people in the Rochester community. She came to the city in the 1970s to assist her daughter Mitzi in caring for her children. Grandma was a tall, thin, regal-looking grey-haired lady who lived most of her life in Texas. Though her Texas drawl faded somewhat after two decades in Rochester, she never lost her love of her home state. She often took winter visits back home and asked that I visit her there. Because of my work with Kay Iwatta Associates, that was easy to do, as I was often asked to facilitate groups for companies on the West Coast. I could go early or come back to Rochester by way of Texas and spend a few days with Grandma. She exposed me America's African-American roots in Texas and took me to museums and cultural organizations that thoroughly invigorated me.

Grandma was one of those women who embraced the whole community. After becoming a member of the Nineteenth Ward Community Association, she worked with children, including our own, to develop their creativity by making Christmas and other holiday gifts for their parents and taught any women who wanted to learn how to sew, quilt, cook and develop back bone. When any new person came to the community, Grandma made sure they met the "right people." She helped them find a job, get oriented and feel at home. She attended association meetings, where we bonded once I became president.

Grandma was always ready with good advice. When I decided to run for office, she was the first person to write a check for the maximum amount and to ask, "What else can I do?" She gave teas and dinner parties to celebrate seasons, accomplishments and successful projects, or to welcome new arrivals. Once I was elected to city council, she asked me to sponsor her appointment to the zoning board.

Grandma often asked *my* advice, as well, about personal concerns and projects she thought an organization in the community, such as the YMCA or the Al Sigl Center, should undertake. She gave and raised money for these projects. Two of her grandchildren had special needs, so she paid particular attention to and supported those organizations that helped children with special needs.

Grandma and I shared a love of poetry and Christian hymns, as well as the joys of being grandmothers, mothers and wives. Her deceased husband was a United Methodist minister in Texas, and she was a Sunday School teacher and active congregational leader.

A few years before her death, Grandma said to me, "One thing I am not happy about in my life is that I am no longer able to be engaged in lives like yours as much as I would like." She had fought through cancer and other health issues and no longer had her usual stamina. I promised to visit her regularly, and I kept that promise. After lengthy illnesses and losing battles, she decided it was time to die and she asked for God's release. She called her friends and relatives, told them she would soon be leaving them, and passed on her final thoughts. She and I worked prayerfully on how she could pass her time while she waited for God's release. We shared poetry and hymns, and spoke of family and friends. She and I both believed that death was not an end but the beginning of another phase of life. I paid tribute to her at her funeral soon after and will always remember her. She was right that our lives do not end but rather pass into another phase, for often the work I carry on is inspired or in some way shaped by her, and I pass that on to others who will carry on after I am gone.

Hattie Harris

Hattie, a staunch Republican, was one of my civic influences, you might say. Known as the Mayor of Strathallan Park, Hattie was the child of poor immigrant Jewish parents who made their living in the Rochester community by selling vegetables from a cart throughout poor neighborhoods. Hattie often accompanied her father on these trips in what we call the third and ninth wards of the city, which she came to know well. I don't remember Hattie mentioning her mother, sisters and brothers, except the brother who lived in France.

Hattie was a strong-minded, clever woman who had great political insight. She often shared with me how many votes she could guarantee a candidate who wanted to be elected to community boards and government. When I asked my colleagues on city council about this claim, they all shrugged their shoulders and said, "Who wants to challenge her?"

All I know is that many of the Republican judges, county legislators, district attorneys and council members not only swore by Hattie's powers, but often paid her tribute by inviting her to important party gatherings, celebrating her birthdays with elaborate parties, and forming a group of men who called themselves "Hattie's Boys." Her "boys" often serenaded her on special occasions.

Hattie had a habit of commanding your presence for lunch, dinner or a chat, and you felt you needed to respond positively. Shortly after I was sworn in as a Rochester City Council member in 1977, Hattie summoned me to visit and have lunch with her in her upstairs Strathallan Park apartment. Reportedly, Hattie owned the whole house, but was content to live on the top floor. Some called it a sign of her being in control and above everyone else. I would have visited her anyway, because as a city-wide council member, I felt it was my responsibility to learn all I could about the whole city and my constituents, whether they voted for me or not. This first visit began a delightful friendship that included my husband, Bill, and our children until Hattie died in her 90s more than two decades later.

She was a regal-looking woman whose countenance revealed her Jewish heritage. She sat in a beautiful straight-backed chair with her hands resting on the arms as if she were a queen. She was dressed in a long silver brocaded gown with comfortable-looking black slippers. She looked me over and asked me to have a seat. She asked if I knew who she was as though I should have known. I told her I had heard of her, but didn't know much about who she was. She said, "I invited you to my house before you became a council member, but you didn't come."

I sat there searching my memory and recalled that we had a brief conversation at a cultural fair on the grounds of the Rochester Museum & Science Center some years back; but I admitted I did not remember the substance of our conversation. Hattie seemed to appreciate that I would admit my memory lapse.

She showed me around her apartment. It was filled with family memorabilia. She told stories of a loose-knit organization she operated to help people around the world escape oppressive governments. In some cases, coded messages giving directions to "safe houses" were smuggled to people who made their way to freedom in the United States. During World War II she said she buried special gifts like food and cigarettes among the grounds inside a coffee can. She thought the cans passed inspection because they weighed the same as a full can of coffee.

During this first of my many visits with Hattie, someone stopped by to see how she was getting along. This woman briefly shared with me what a wonderful woman Hattie was.

Before long, Hattie got to the subject of her summons of me to her apartment. There was talk of building the Strathallan Hotel at the end of her block which, she thought, would be the beginning of hotels nestled into a number of the city's neighborhoods. Such hotels were common in other cities throughout the country and Europe. Hattie was fearful that the hotel would not be in good taste and would ruin the nearby East Avenue. Rochesterians were proud of the mansions that lined that street including the home of Kodak founder George Eastman.

My only promise to her that day, as often was the case with constituents, was that I would look into it and tell her what I thought, and if I did not agree with her assessment, I would support the development. I also would visit the developers of the project and determine if I felt their plans were consistent with this highly esteemed neighborhood. Between those meetings and my colleagues on city council, I felt that I would support the development and reported back to Hattie. She was not pleased and told me so in the tone of the short queen who rises to her full height and says, "We are not pleased."

In order to soothe the situation, I did go back to the developers and suggest that they really needed to make peace with Hattie. To make a long story short, the original owners named the top-floor bar and dance floor "Hattie's." Hattie entertained there and felt honored by the designation for a number of years, until she had a disagreement with the owners. She then grew less enchanted with the designation and asked that her name be removed. Several renovations and years later, what had become a late-night jazz scene closed and Hattie moved from the city.

Some say her move was prompted by her announcement in 1985 that she was considering a candidacy for mayor. Most of the opinion makers had not viewed Hattie in this light and made fun of the idea. I personally thought she would have been a great mayor, but I knew the odds would be stacked against her.

When I ran for mayor eight years later, Hattie—ailing and no longer a city resident—lamented that she could not ensure my election with her now-waning power brought on partly by illness. Our relationship grew into a friendship in which she as the aging philosopher mentored me, her pupil. We discussed and compared our early lives, our parents and our faith. She was estranged from her local synagogue and I encouraged her not to give up her faith for any person. I understand that she eventually rejoined, but never verified that.

Clementine Cherry Balkum

Clementine Cherry's face was a round, bright tan, inviting visage. Her eyes sparkled like the stars and she always had a smile. The artist in me recalls her face as a wonderful subject to be captured by one more talented than I.

I do not recall when Bill and I first met her, but it was probably at a community meeting about schools, their deficiencies and the violence that, in the early 1970s, festered in the community and spilled into the schools. Mrs. Cherry had seven children whom she raised alone after her husband was claimed by street violence in the 1960s in Rochester.

Mrs. Cherry became a parent representative in the Title I Program developed to assure that poor and minority parents had access to educational opportunities and training. The parent boards actually had input into the running of the programs, which local school boards organized. More important, they had input into the evaluation of those programs and could insist that outcomes and weaknesses of the programs be a part of federal reporting. I watched this program develop more activism among local parents, some of whom ran successfully for school board and ran campaigns for other school board candidates who supported and revamped programs when necessary.

During the early 1970s, as a trainer and advisor for schools for Title I requirements, I often counseled parents such as Mrs. Cherry on how to hold the system accountable for the education of their children. They often met with me for strategy sessions, moral support and debriefing. Later, when I became a city official myself, we held the same type of sessions related to city and other government services.

It was my contention, and still is, that public trust is best served by making sure all neighborhoods receive the best service possible with the dollars spent and that no one neighborhood should take priority because of party affiliation or the financial status of its citizens. It seems to me that elected officials have a responsibility to all neighborhoods regardless of their voting records or political proclivity. This commitment sometimes put me at odds with those who felt that power should be used to benefit those who were already "connected" and well off or those who agreed with the political persuasion of the ones in power.

The most amazing contribution that Clementine Cherry made to my political career and our personal lives was her special commitment to my mother, who developed Alzheimer's when she lived with us and our children. Whatever Clementine felt was necessary to make my life easier—from cleaning my house to cooking meals to accompanying the family on trips to sharing a hotel room with Mom—was carried out by her with limited remuneration and absolute loyalty. She would simply call me on the phone and say, "I think you need my help. How can I help you in supporting the community, because we need you!" She was obviously in one of those "circles" that God drew for us, despite having seven children of her own.

She also mentored younger women who had some of the same struggles in life that she had encountered. She had a strong faith in God and though, to my knowledge, she did not formally belong to a church, she practiced Christianity without compromise or apology. The words to the old song, *And They'll Know We Are Christians By Our Love*, must have been referring to Mrs. Cherry. She often quoted Biblical verses such as "Do unto others what you would have them do unto you," "God is not mocked," "Whatsoever a man soweth, that shall he also reap," "The Lord is my Shepherd, I shall not want," "Nothing shall separate me from the love of God which is in Christ Jesus."

She would often say to me, "I know God has something good in store for me if I just remain faithful to his word and hold to his unchanging hand."

She taught her children to be good citizens and to be community-conscious by example. They followed in her footsteps. She and Bill had a great partnership with her children, as Bill did with many other parents' children. He provided inspiration and correction for them as he encountered them in school, and mothers like Mrs. Cherry provided the "at home" foundation for youth whose encounters they shared.

In the late 1990s, Mrs. Cherry married Robert Balkum, a tall, handsome, dark-skinned gentleman with an obvious adoration for her. They were able, with some advice and help, to purchase a home only several blocks away from our house. It was a just reward for a life well lived that Mr. B. and she found each other and just the right home where she could beautify her yard with flowers. I particularly appreciated her efforts to beautify the community through the planting of flowers in her own yard—another great role model. You could always tell which home was occupied by Clementine Balkum and her family.

Drawn Into the Political Circle

Bill and I were drawn into political life without realizing it. Our volunteer work led to my selection by the Democratic Party as a delegate to the 1975 Democratic Convention in New York City. Bill was an alternate. I remember Barbara Jordan's keynote address that riveted the audience and sparked calls for her nomination as the next vice presidential candidate. My parents received calls from friends who had seen my intense expression as the network news cameras panned the audience.

Jimmy Carter was selected as the presidential candidate. I had been asked by the party to represent Mo Udall, whose vision for America's future captivated me, but my leaning was toward Carter. I was all too happy when he won the nomination.

The Carters held a reception for delegates and we were pleased to meet both Rosalynn and Jimmy. How receptive he was to new ideas and common people! I applauded his appointment of Ron Brown, the first African-American secretary of commerce. I promised Ron that, as a member of the Board of Directors of the National League of Cities, I would join a delegation on an international business development mission, but before that trip could unfold, he was killed on a trip to the Middle East. His staff reported that he had a gunshot to the head even though the plane reportedly crashed in a storm.

When we returned home to Rochester, Bill and I began to work on the Carter campaign. Midge Costanza, Rochester's at-large city council member, traveled across the country with presidential hopeful Carter as an Easterner to balance his own Southern support. When Carter was elected, he appointed Midge to his cabinet-level staff, creating a vacancy in her council seat. Because of my position as president of the Nineteenth Ward Association, Democratic Committeewoman Kathy Sette urged me to run for her seat. I had no intention of running, but after her encouragement and their challenge to "see if the selection process is fair," I decided to run. That started my political career so many years ago.

With a number of ordinary people from across the country, I was invited to the White House for a Carter think-tank session on how to jump start the city economies. It was there on the veranda of the White House that I reconnected with a childhood friend (twin Beverly Thompson Wooten) who had lived down the street from me on Ann Street and been one of the attendants at our wedding in Albion. She was also an invitee for the Urban Session. See what circles God draws!

One of my major interests was in the federal government allowing the sale of development bonds in the free market and giving development grants rather than the program grants previous administrations had been so fond of providing to state governments to then share with cities (after taking the state administrative cut). It was my and the league's position that direct aid to cities would be in order because locals had different problems and best knew how to craft solutions. We also pushed that these grants be given through the Department of Housing and Urban Development.

Later, the whole family was invited to have lunch with the Carters in the private suites quarters during an Easter vacation. We traveled to D.C. with excitement and anticipation of an opportunity for the children to play with daughter Amy in her tree house. When we arrived, we were escorted to the living quarters by one of the private family aids and presented with a note of regret from the Carter family that they could not be present to greet us, but felt the need for some family time. Subsequently, the news confirmed that the hostage crisis was heating up in the Middle East, the presidential family needed to take a vacation together before the storm broke. A failed attempt was made to rescue the hostages when the American Embassy was taken over by militants. However, the highlight of that visit for the children was getting to play in Amy's tree house. Our highlight was to see the living quarters and to have been invited. We keep saying we want to visit the Carter Center for International Peace and the church in Plains, Georgia where we are told Jimmy Carter still occasionally teaches Sunday School. Guess whose father was born in Waycross, Georgia? Yes, mine. Another circle, perhaps? Then, as a result of Carter's choice for urban advisor, Midge Costanza, I was appointed with her blessing to fill the at-large seat of City Council for Rochester, New York.

The subsequent chapter of our relationship with the Carter family unfolded around my role as the co-chair of the 51.3 Committee for Monroe County during his second run for the White House. The Census projections for country in 1979 were an indication that for the first time in the history of the country, women were a majority. Thus, the Democratic National Committee organized 51.3 committees to engage and get out the women's vote. That is why President Carter called our

Photo from one of the yearly postcards I received from the Carters.

Sue Leone, campaign worker.

home on the eve of the election to ask how he was doing in Monroe County and I had to share with him the sad news that it looked like he would carry the city, but not the county.

"Well," he said, "you did a great job, and I thank you." Not a very consoling conversation up to the level of our previous encounters, but treasured, memorable words. Bill and I believe it was the national news stations counting the days of failure to rescue the hostages that really led to the Carter defeat in his second run for the presidency. But what a decent, wonderful and worldwide respected Nobel Laureate he is.

We had met Maya Angelo, my daughter Crystal's favorite poet, at the swearing in of President Carter and had a brief conversation with her. We met again (she and Crystal bonded immediately) at the home of the Spelman College President Johnetta Coles when attending the graduation of our first niece, Kheri Holland. Her dad, Bob—my oldest brother and former president of Ben and Jerry's—was then president of the Spelman Board of Directors. I had long enjoyed Maya's books, especially, *I Know Why the Caged Bird Sings*. We talked with her about her writing and the poetry she composed for the swearing-in of Jimmy Carter. She encouraged me and Crystal to keep writing. Her insight about being driven by our muse to write was encouraging. I met and talked with Maya again when attending a Leadership America meeting where she was the keynote speaker. She urged women to take their rightful roles in the world and to create more beauty as a responsibility. Our paths have continued to cross over the years. Like me, she "never meets a stranger."

Shortly after attending the Spelman graduation ceremony, Leadership America had a session at Spelman where President Coles was our keynote speaker. She had already shared with me and Bill the challenges of being the first female president of a major Southern college. There were few women presidents of colleges, particularly in the South. Therefore, she formed a President's Forum to share challenges and strategies for running their respective institutions. Her talk to us and with us at Leadership America was an urging of women to seek more significant roles in higher education, as well as heads of companies and governments. "We women bring not only significant skills, but important insight to direct and guide all kinds of organizations." "We must use those gifts to bring about better institutions, a better society and a better world." It was at this meeting that I also learned that my brother Bob was instrumental in her being chosen as president of Spelman, and their friendship was strong enough to include me as a member of the relationship. It was during her and Bob's tenure at Spelman that the Bill and Camille Cosby family gave the largest gift that had ever been given to the college, and they built a beautiful art museum.

Bill and I visited that museum while attending the 1993 Olympics in Atlanta. The museum's first floor is reserved for traveling exhibits, many of which, we understand, are arranged in maze-like fashion so that one feels, as well as sees, the experience of the exhibit. We also were invited to reside in the president's campus apartment while she and her family moved to their family home in Atlanta. Circles, circles, circles. The multi-artist exhibit that was there when we visited was the experience of the African-American family from slavery to the present time, with projections to the future. It was an emotional, exhilarating journey through both the Olympics and that exhibit.

The Nineteenth Ward Community Association was the strongest neighborhood association in Rochester in the early 1970s. Adventures as president of the association led me to be engaged with many of the city's neighborhood associations. We formed a loose-knit group to keep city services throughout our neighborhood and readily addressed deficits and problems before the city council and mayor on a regular basis.

As chair of the youth committee, I hired Tom Argust, a community minister from Detroit, to head a youth services project working with West High School, now Wilson High Commencement Park.

The National Institute of Mental Health awarded us the only grant to a neighborhood group. Our proposal was to deter our youth from being caught up in the court system. We collaborated with West High School. Our goal was to demonstrate how professional services should be for troubled youth and then get out of the business of providing a professional service. In addition to being chosen by the strongest neighborhood association as the city as president, that presidency placed me as a delegate to National Neighbors, a consortium of associations across the nation funded by the Ford Foundation. That body elected me as president and I traveled across the country advising groups on how and when to challenge political processes that hurt their neighborhoods.

Kathy and Jerry O'Neill were key in my run for office because their contribution was to care for our children whenever we needed them. Jerry was a master photographer, available whenever I needed him, and Kathy supplied me with light reading to relax.

Honorable Assemblyman David Gant and County Legislator Tony Reed in my campaign office for mayor, plotting strategy.

My two campaign managers, Kathy Sette and me at a rally for Congresswoman Louise Slaughter. My mayoral campaign manager, Gaynelle Wethers, is behind Kathy. She kept my spirits up for a long and arduous run for mayor as I fought for the appointment among six candidates.

Bill and me with sister-in-law Claudia at a political celebration.

Bill and me with Senator Ralph Quattrociocchi.

Ron Thomas, Cynthia Elliott, me and another campaign worker.

Bill and me at a sesquicentennial event in 1984.

Bill and me.

Joyce Herman and the Honorable County Manager Lucien Morin at a panel discussion at a community forum at St. Mary's Church downtown. County Manager Morin later presented me with the Monroe County Medal of Honor for community service.

Senator Daniel Patrick Moynihan's public forum during Rochester's City Living week celebration in City Council Chambers with me, Councilwoman Joan Hensler, Mayor Thomas P. Ryan and Councilwoman Lois Geiss.

Planting trees with neighborhood residents and the mayor.

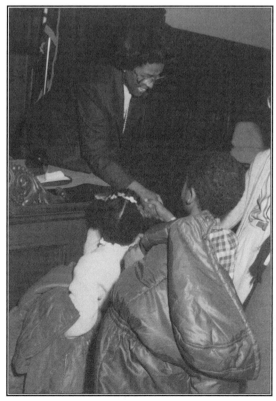

Welcoming Rochester children as president of city council.

Consulting with my "kitchen cabinet," the children of Rochester.

Public Service and City Council

As soon as we moved into the Nineteenth Ward, the Neighborhood Association was right at our door to enlist our membership. After being on the Council of Delegates of the Nineteenth Ward Association as a delegate for our area, I was appointed by Al Sette to be the chair of the youth committee. He and his wife, Kathy, nominated me for president of the association as the first woman and first African-American to hold that office. The Republican Party's future mayor, Samuel May, and Democratic Party Mayor Frank Lamb, a neighbor from Genesee Park Boulevard, invited us to their homes for coffee as they campaigned for our allegiance.

This was exciting to us because politics and controversial or complex discussion in the town of Delevan had been simply nonexistent. Rochester's stirring social and political issues reawakened in us the fires we hadn't stirred since our young adult years. I recall that in Delevan, about 40 miles south of Buffalo, our coroner/town undertaker, Claris Parsons, would change his party membership periodically just to see if his office would be held—and it always was.

Both major Rochester parties were in the throes of leadership challenges from younger members. The Democrats determined that a new day had dawned and leadership changes were necessary in order to move the party and the city forward. Besides, all of the jobs went to Republicans as long as they were in office. Everything from construction to taxicab licenses was held by Republican families and passed down as inheritances and even entitlements. The young Republicans, on the other hand, were challenging the status quo in their party.

Bill's mother had been a Republican County Committee member in White Plains. My father was an avid, but critical, Democrat who became a councilmember in Albion, Michigan, during my college days. As far as Dad was concerned, there was no other party. After all, as a student of history, he bought the theory that Lincoln's freeing of the slaves was more of a move to save the Union than a humanitarian gesture. It was, for him, a foregone conclusion that many of the riots after World War II were sparked by bigots unchecked by Republican administrations and that black WWII veterans were blocked from buying houses under the GI Bill of Rights.

It seemed to Bill and me that the Democratic Party offered more possibility of openness and making a contribution to the community. We arrived in Rochester after the city's riots of 1964 and although the winds of change had not yet manifested themselves fully, there was a compelling sense of urgency in our local political activities. We, too, had lived through the whirlwind Kennedy days and were inspired by President Lyndon Johnson's War on Poverty, then depressed by the national turn of events after he built up involvement in Vietnam. Later, through a series of elections, socially conservative Republicans wrestled the control of that party from the more socially sensitive and liberal (dare we use the word) party members.

We joined the Democratic Party, the Nineteenth Ward Neighborhood Association and the nearby United Methodist Church at Post Avenue and Sawyer Street. When we lived in Delevan, Bill met the Rev. Gene Ferguson at the Western New York Conference of the United Methodist Church Quadrennial Emphasis Committee in Buffalo. When we came to Rochester, Gene and his wife, Joy, offered us a place in their home until we found housing. They became our perennial bridge partners and still are. During bridge, we solve all the problems of the world. It was Gene who pointed out to us that part of the racial tension in the Nineteenth Ward was a misunderstanding. When "block busting" was rampant, whites were being urged by Realtors to sell their houses even if they took a loss to get out before the "blacks" moved in and lowered property values. The Nineteenth Ward Neighborhood Association strategized placing signs in the windows of neighborhood homes saying, "We're staying," meaning, "We're not afraid that you (blacks) are moving into the neighborhood. We welcome you as neighbors and we are staying."

Some blacks, anxious to purchase good housing, misinterpreted those signs to mean, "We are staying and you cannot buy our house."

Hearing about that misunderstanding enabled Bill and me to build some bridges by being interpreters of the intent of both black and white neighbors across the Rochester community.

When Gene and Joy were moved by the church's district superintendent to Kenmore near Buffalo, our spirits led Bill and I to Memorial A.M. E. Zion Church. We were drawn there by the social gospel lived by the minister, the Rev. Andrew Gibson and the historical nature of the church—Frederick Douglass, Harriet Tubman and Susan B. Anthony found crossroads there in their struggles for women's suffrage and civil rights. Additionally, we were drawn by the music and the friendly greetings given our family every time we visited the church. We felt like we were being welcomed home. Mr. and Mrs. Bullock were the chief greeters. Mrs. Bullock was the unofficial church historian, along with Chuck Frazier, who enriched our knowledge of the greater Rochester community and this church, which was established before Rochester became a village. She became such an intimate part of our circle that when Mother came a few years later to help raise the children while I served on city council, they became fast friends. We continue to enjoy her wealth of knowledge and special wit that few 99-year-olds can express. Her friendship is one of our life's treasures.

Mother came to live with us in 1977 after my first council appointment to help care for our children. They were delighted to have Grandmother share their everyday lives. I was equally happy to have my best confidante and friend in our household.

As new educators in Rochester, Bill and I were welcomed by groups of Rochesterians trying to piece together a more cohesive community following the riots of the mid-1960s. Catherine Carlson, daughter of the inventor of the photocopier that made Xerox Corporation an international company; Betty and Bob Strasenburgh; and several others invited us to focus groups where we talked about the possibility of forming a community foundation, the new movement sweeping the country to support community efforts beyond social services as building community. Groups of whites who wanted to adopt or had adopted biracial children sought our advice on raising "healthy" children. Multicultural groups such as Citizens of Quality Integrated Education (CQIE) and faith-based groups seeking more informed understanding of the racial divide sought our conversational advice.

The Rev. Oprah Francis, one of few African-American female clergy, engaged me in finding and funding a "safe house" for women and their children seeking to leave the streets. I was asked to join with founders of the Equal Educational Opportunity Center, an arm of the State University of New York at Brockport, to improve minority and poor city school district children's college success.

Dr. Marjorie Scott; Dave Henderson, executive director; Dr. Elizabeth Mills, counselor; I and many others developed a strategic plan to open the center, which still exists in Rochester. I also remember Garth Fagan, renowned award-winning choreographer, being in our discussions. His dance troupe, Garth Fagan Dance, then was known as the Bottom of the Bucket, But. (Garth was once asked about his dance troupe and replied, "Well, to tell you the truth, they're the bottom of the bucket, but ...") Our link to this professional dance troupe formed part of our circle in the arts in Rochester and also with Steve Humphrey, whose mother, Lillian, was one of my first close friends in Rochester. I knew her about two years. Steve's mother was dying of cancer when he was just a high school senior. Lillian expressed her concern to me about what would happen to her son when she died. I shared this conversation with Garth and he replied, "Tell Lillian she does not need to worry about her son. I will take care of him and he is going to be a fine dancer."—And he is.

On arriving in Rochester, we jumped into our new roles. Bill and I got involved in stuffing envelopes and manning telephones at the Democratic Party headquarters during the spring and fall of 1969. There, we met Larry Kirwin, future party chairman, and David Gant, future dean of the Rochester Delegation to New York's state capital at Albany, as well as other notable Democrats, Tom Fink, master fundraiser (who was my finance chair in three of my four runs for office); Louise Slaughter, now the dean of the state delegation to Washington; and Tom Fry, Democratic County executive in 1988. Connie and John Mitchell were the only other blacks, besides David Gantt, whom we remember having extensive conversations with as we volunteered at party headquarters. Needless to say, the camaraderie there allowed us to unconsciously and unintentionally take measure of many of our future colleagues and opponents. We were encouraged to become poll watchers and eventually poll workers when we realized the Democratic Party, with its low enrollment, had trouble getting people to represent them in all of the political functions.

It was not long before Bill and I were well known in the Democratic Party. I was asked to finish the city council term of Midge Costanza, who was appointed by Jimmy Carter as Assistant to the President for Public Liaison in 1976. I did not know at the time I accepted that I would continue in political life as I found it a useful position to mitigate the challenges that I believed faced Rochester. Midge's term as at-large city council member was enough to teach me how to use the tools of public service.

After I was appointed to city council, there were a number of people who filled my breakfast, lunch and dinner calendar so that people could tell me what they do, as well as what I could do for them. The three most memorable meetings were Jim McCuller, head of ABC—Action For a Better Community; a construction company president; and community visionary Joe Posner. The meeting with Jim laid a foundation for us working together during my council years to provide services to the inner city and to know when the services were not being adequately rendered to neighborhoods. Jim kept me informed; however, that first meeting was a little testy. He said, "I don't know who you are. People are asking me and since I am the leader in the black community, I need to know more about you."

As the conversation went on, I became somewhat uncomfortable. I said, "I am not sure what you are asking, but I don't bow down to anybody but God."

Jim often spoke in hyperbole. He said, "Everybody bows down to somebody,"

I replied, "You don't look like it."

He said, "Touché."

I did admire the political training he provided for his constituents who came through his ABC programs. He and I decided to respect our different leadership styles that we each had in serving some of the same constituents.

In the second memorable incident, a builder approached me with an offer to provide discounted services and surplus house furnishings. I told him I was not comfortable with that. He tried to push me by saying everybody does, but I firmly declined. My father's warning bells went off. I remember my mom told me a construction company dumped surplus crushed stone in our driveway one night when Dad was a councilman. They were hoping to curry favor with him, but he called them late that night to remove it as he did not want even a hint of impropriety.

Anyone who knew Joe Posner, founder of the Rochester Area Community Foundation, knew that if he invited you to breakfast, you were going to be brought into one of his projects. If you tried to decline, saying you have no time, he would offer to help you find the time. I was one of those who could not resist his crusade when he proposed a project called Quad A, a program that through sports education enrichment, sought to support poor youth in our community to make contributions to the world. He and I shared a belief in the importance of treating youth as heirs to the future.

A groundswell of requests from the Nineteenth Ward members urged me to apply for the seat left vacant by Midge Costanza. The majority of Democrats would choose the replacement, who was also a Democrat, from an interview process established for identifying candidates by the city committee chairs of the party.

Party Chairman Larry Kirwin asked, "Why are you doing this? I know your family can't afford to finance your campaign. Wait your turn and I can assure you a district seat next election. The city is not ready for an African-American being a citywide councilmember. Besides, I have already promised the next vacant seat to someone."

I asked if it was Connie Mitchell. He said no.

I declined to withdraw. If he had said "Connie," I would have withdrawn, recognizing her significant leadership during Rochester's critical civil-rights struggles.

The committee recommended two people! They submitted both my name and the name Larry Kirwin wanted. It was actually a surprise to Bill and me when the seat was offered with the provision that I would have to leave my city school district job to accept their appointment, run in a few months, and again a year and a half later.

Bill and I always used an intensive private process to arrive at decisions for the family. Using an easel and writing points of discussion, we turned the issues around in our minds. We listed pros and cons. One consideration was that, by then, Crystal was four and I would not be at home for her entry into kindergarten as I had for each of our other two children. Considering the struggles ahead, we finally decided it was too good an opportunity to give up. Bill said it was my decision to make. He would support me 100%—and he did.

How I Got to City Council

Bill and I arrived in Rochester after the riots of 1964 exposed some of the challenging issues that faced the city. The Rev. Franklin Florence stated that the three main challenges facing the city were education, housing and employment. Despite all of our work as a whole, today's 21st century depressed economy maintains those challenges as education, housing and employment. I personally pushed for remediation and solutions of these challenges through every opportunity that presented itself to the council and initiated many programs and projects. At times these initiatives required a major push against fellow county and city elected officials who were concerned with the public perceptions and established power centers in the county and city. Local African-Americans who were excluded from all but menial jobs at Kodak, Xerox, and Bausch & Lomb, were almost nonexistent in city hall. The only African-American employed at city hall was an elevator operator.

Councilmember Chris Lindley urged me to the League of Cities meetings, where I eventually joined the leadership ranks and served as a board member. Chris was a progressive-minded history professor from the University of Rochester who guarded against favoritism in awarding contracts, represented the public interest in decisions, and did not seem threatened, as some male members did, when the balance of council members shifted to five women and four men. One of the women, Jean Carozzi, took Charlie Schiano's seat as the lone Republican. She was not only cooperative, she often proposed good legislation. Perhaps the fact that I received the highest number of votes in the Charlotte neighborhood, a traditionally Republican stronghold, held some sway in the cooperation of her party on council.

The local newspaper reported: "A black woman from the Southwest has been chosen to fill the unexpired term of a white Italian woman from the Northeast. How about that!" My first campaign motto was "Ruth Scott Brings People Together."

New circles began to form in our lives. Bill jokingly indicated there should be an elected officials' spouses' club and made friends with circles that included the spouses. Bill was more than a political asset. He was my secret source of encouragement, power and a steady ear to listen to my analytical conclusions of issues—my chief sounding board. When we visited the male-dominated committees, associations and churches for their approval, the men would take him aside to say, "Do you really approve of this?" Bill would say, "Wholeheartedly! She will be the greatest council member!" It was those same men who gave "permission" for women in their households to sign petitions.

My main goal as council member was to promote community and fairness for all.

We fired the city manager during my second year as a council member for lack of confidence because the press often knew what was going on at City Hall before we did. Mayor Lamb decided to retire, and camera-shy Tom Ryan became mayor. Since I had garnered the most votes of any on the "at-large" slate, I was offered the position of vice mayor but felt it might take me away from Bill and our children too much.

I set out early in my council terms to empower city neighborhoods and black churches to work together to solve several common problems. I worked with Josh Lofton in the city schools, volunteered with the Rochester Area Community Foundation grants committee and worked with city libraries to mediate turf wars between white and black city youth.

My second priority was to enlighten myself about the inner workings of city departments. I found secretaries, as well as department heads, most willing to share their needs and concerns.

From these visits arose another priority—gaining access to city jobs and contracts for minorities. With the collaboration of district Councilmember Ron Good, also African-American, I discovered that African-American males were required to clock in at the Department of Public Works facilities at three o'clock in the morning in hope of getting a substitute position when someone did not show up for work. The records of their attendance for a "chance" to work were proof of their commitment. We proposed and the council accepted, after considerable discussion and legal analysis, to retroactively include these men in the pension system offering both jobs and family health benefits. They were rewarded for their faithful attendance. That was a proud accomplishment for me, as well as fulfillment of purpose.

At a time when there were very few elected women and minorities across the country, caucuses were formed in national organizations, all of which helped in my growth as a leader. I went to the League of Cities and reconnected with those circles of former friends and colleagues from my social and church background in Cleveland.

Among the people I reconnected with were Councilman Ronald Gant, my cousin from Albion, Michigan; friends from Cleveland social and church circles; former National Neighbors presidents, all of them fulfilling their commitment to change the world through their public service. Among them was Mayor Jackson from Atlanta. He had been the keynote speaker at my swearing in as president of the Nineteenth Ward in Rochester.

Some council members from Indiana and Illinois asked, "Are you related to Bob Holland?" It turned out that Dad was well-known in Masonic circles throughout these communities for his oratory as he presided over numerous rituals in the Masonic community. As a 33rd Degree Mason, he was the keynote speaker and leader of rituals at many events.

My first campaign was aided by Midge Costanza's support after the appointment even though I learned later that a friend of hers had been promised the seat. It was from her I got the line, "Some people love to run. Others love to serve. I love both." She campaigned with me at the public market, and the weekend before the election, our pictures were on the front page of the Sunday *New York Times*. Her other gift to me was introducing me to her personal shopper, Pamela, of Pamela's Dress Shop on East Avenue. Pamela and I had several sessions in which she helped me organize my wardrobe and fill in items needed so I could always be press-ready. My friend Gwen Martins assumed that role when I ran for mayor.

Mayor Tom Ryan's major sayings were "No surprises" and "Let's disagree agreeably."

I had no problem buying into those protocols as long as there was mutual access to cooperation and policy formation. Tom was dedicated and very private. Helping him become more comfortable with public appearances and hopefully dispel the media jokes about "Mumbles Tom" helped him be more comfortable in public. I said, "If you will visit neighborhood meetings and in-studio press conferences, I will accompany you." I believe this made a significant contribution to his comfort with moving over to the directly elected strong mayor as the charter was amended in 1984. I became the first president of the newly elected Rochester City Council.

When I came to Rochester, we had a city manager form of government with a nine-member city council—four district seats and five at-large seats. Midge Costanza had been the only woman on council and an at-large member.

I was very interested in improving housing and community services. Joan Hensler and I developed legislation to make an exception to the zoning law that prohibited more than three unrelated people from living in an R-1 (residential) zone. The intent of the law was to prevent houses from being converted to rooming houses as some in the poorer neighborhoods had been. The effect was that churches were prevented from offering services in communities where their mission could be most effective. The Catholic nuns were unable to live in groups of three or more in single-family houses in R-1 neighborhoods outside of the convent. I also proposed legislation to allow churches to purchase and develop vacant property from the city to provide non-discriminating social services to youth and adults. Most of these buildings were in black neighborhoods. All members of the council, except Chris Lindley and I, were Catholic, so I reminded other members of their willingness to allow variances for the Catholic Diocese and that this same privilege should be extended to Protestant churches that have a stable history of providing social services to their neighbors.

As a result of this new policy I championed, in 1990, just after my retirement from council, Zion Hill Missionary Baptist Church on Samuel McCree Way built a new building from which it provided drug

I continued to serve after leaving city council by being a consultant to Frederick Douglass Village established by the Rev. Errol Bunt, pastor of Memorial A.M.E. Zion Church. We built 27 low- to moderate-income houses on two new streets. It was the first such individually owned housing project by African-Americans in the City of Rochester.

We made instant friends with Bob and Vivian Alexander of Pittsford through the
AAVW Couples Cooking Club, although they were serious Republicans. The Alexanders
became not only supportive of my political campaigns, but a second family to welcome
and love our children when we were away from the city. (They also had two girls
and a boy.) The Alexanders organized a cross-cultural cross-country group called The
Adventurers. Even our children envied the fun of our nights out with the group. Bill and
Bob became teaching buddies at Marshall High School. We miss Bob's lively laughter
and vivid political discussions. They made our lives rich in friendship and support.

rehabilitation. Other churches soon developed child development centers, nursery schools and daycare. Three years after leaving Council, I became the chief consultant to Memorial A.M.E. Zion Church in building the first moderate- to low-income housing units, called Frederick Douglass Village. Together with the senior residence called Edwards Manor, this development became the first moderate- to low-income housing units built by African-Americans. My experience in networking helped connect the Rev. Errol Hunt, president and founder of the Frederick Douglass Board, to federal grants, local foundation supporters, city zoning offices and banks.

This city area southwest of the Frederick Douglass/Susan B. Anthony Bridge is adjacent to the rapidly developing Corn Hill Neighborhood. Decades ago, the neighborhood was undergoing gentrification. Some beautiful mansions that once were the homes of Rochester's wealthy businessmen and millers were torn down. Many of the homes that were left were subdivided into rooms to rent or small apartments by absentee landlords. Some original residents remained in their homes. Some poor citizens had been in Corn Hill for generations. I walked door to door to advise the underrepresented residents to hold onto their property until they could get a good price. Many of them sold out to these money-hungry developers who offered three to sixteen thousand dollars cash for the homes, then sold them for fifty to two hundred and fifty thousand dollars—rehabilitated or not. Some property, especially in the southwest corner of the city, had become prime real estate, so the homes that sat on those lots were demolished and new developments sprang up in their places. Preservationists and people who opposed the gentrification that was taking place in the city formed the Landmark Society of Western New York to stop the demolition of Rochester's pioneer mansions. The Corn Hill Neighborhood Association, sister to the Nineteenth Ward Association and the Charlotte Association, drove the process for seeing that the quality of construction remained high.

Politics is Not for the Faint of Heart

When Mayor Thomas P. Ryan, Jr. decided to retire, I gave careful consideration to running myself. My terms on city council had strengthened me, and I felt ready to take on the issues that the city faced from the stronger vantage point of mayor, which by this time had become a strong mayor form of government rather than city manager. Two issues, in particular, served to strengthen me.

The first was in my first term. Bill and I arrived in Rochester after the riots of 1964, but many of the issues that led to them were still smoldering under the surface, unseen by the public and seemingly unaddressed by the city government. The issue of police brutality, particularly in the black community, was a growing debate. A coalition of concerned citizens was clamoring for police brutality incidents to go to a civilian review board as in many other cities across the nation.

In my first year on city council, a meeting was called by this coalition at the Central Church of Christ. Mayor Ryan was asked to address the meeting but he declined. As a council member, I insisted that the coalition's invitation be accepted. As head of the city council, the mayor and other council members looked to me as the chair of the Public Safety Committee to attend the meeting. I accepted with the provision that my recommendations would be accepted by council.

Bill and I attended the meeting on a stiflingly hot summer evening.

The church was overflowing with standing-room only. I soon realized that the anger of the crowd would have likely erupted into more violent demonstrations if the issues were ignored. Some people complained that when women in the black community called the police, those women often ended up killed by police gunfire. As I now recall, we had two such incidents in that summer.

A second complaint was that reports of police misconduct were often swept under the rug through internal police department investigations. Citizens were intimidated by the complaint intake process and by officers responsible for the complaint. The internal review reports following "officer gunfire resulting in the death of a citizen" were secretly held with no public input or review. These reports were protected under the state laws as they related to personnel files. Even the city council and mayor were uninformed. The citizen anger seemed to me to be more justifiable given the lack of governmental or police response or even awareness of the community's issues.

The meeting, run by the Rev. Franklin Florence, an outspoken, respected leader in the black community, grew more intense. Citizens were angry that the mayor had not thought enough of their issues to attend the meeting.

Rev. Franklin had to quiet the murmuring crowd by saying, "Councilwoman Scott has come. Let's hear what she has to say."

I first expressed sympathy for those families who had experienced mishandling of domestic disputes and other brutalities under our police force. I told the crowd in no uncertain terms that the citizen review board that was desired could not be achieved, but I would work to craft some solutions that would be evaluated by city council and made public.

I had done my homework for this meeting. I studied other cities where a civilian review board had been put into place. Where civilian control boards had been tried, the same problems appeared. As the meeting went on, I thought dialogue between the public and city government, as well as a lack of transparency of police proceedings, were additionally unaddressed, and maybe even unidentified, issues. I also knew we in the city government had to develop a step-by-step process for addressing these problems. I proposed and the council adopted videotaping the police input process and using those tapes for police training and for public review.

Under my plan, rather than a citizen review board, a council member would be placed on a review committee with one other appointed person from the Center for Dispute Settlement. City council would review the data publicly on a quarterly basis and make whatever changes were needed in the police department to address unresolved issues. A corollary to the plan was mandatory training for officers in ways to de-escalate violence in family disputes instead of drawing guns. With much contentious discussion with the police union and the public at large, the plan was adopted and is known in dispute resolution circles and the police training academy as the "Ruth Scott Solution" for settling police controversy.

The second controversial issue occurred when I became city council president. Across America, churches were providing safe havens for political dissidents from South America, particularly at this time El Salvador. The city council was asked to declare Rochester a "Sanctuary City." I gathered information from mayors and council presidents through the League of Cities and determined that Rochester should consider it. It seemed a natural progression of previous adoptions, such as the ban on city government purchases from Northern Ireland and South Africa (proposed by Maxine Childress Brown).

I called the Immigration Office in Buffalo to gather more information from them as I formulated my proposal to the council. Then, to my surprise, followed a string of intimidations and threatening phone calls. I and other council members received veiled threats strongly suggesting that we had no right to even consider such an ordinance and that we would be prosecuted with the full force of the federal government's authority if we persisted.

I kept an open mind as to whether I would, in the end, vote for the proposal, but I was determined that it would get a full public hearing. When representatives from immigration appeared at our meeting, they insisted on meeting with the lone Republican council member before meeting with the whole council. They repeated their absolute intention to sue the city and prosecute anyone voting for such a measure in what they called "a violation federal statutes," though they did not and probably could not name these statutes.

The actions of the federal immigration agents the evening before the scheduled vote confirmed my affirmation of the proposal.

At this time, the Prebysterian Church across Fitzhugh Street across from city hall, was providing sanctuary in the church for an El Salvadorian couple. One evening after midnight, the couple went for a walk on the nearby Sister City Bridge in downtown Rochester. Immigration agents waiting patiently for this opportunity swooped down upon them with guns drawn, arrested the husband and took him to Buffalo for booking. His wife was left standing on the bridge screaming in Spanish. Some citizens heard her and walked her back to the church. She understood no English. I must say I was proud of the Rochester church community that reportedly raised the more than $20,000 bail within hours. The man was released and brought back to Rochester to join his wife. Needless to say, the nine-member council vote was 8-0 with one abstention. Rochester continued the proud traditions of the Underground Railroad, abolitionist Frederick Douglass and women's rights leader Susan B. Anthony when it joined many other cities across America in becoming a "Sanctuary City."

A full analysis of my run for mayor of Rochester would take another whole book. When I left city council in 1989, I became fully immersed in building a successful business and was well on my way when, four years later, Tom Ryan decided to step down after two terms under the strong mayor system. He had already served several terms under the city manager system, making him the longest serving mayor in New York State. I kept within the circle of my family, close friends and colleagues the possibility of my running. I had to ponder whether to place my company on hold or turn it over to one of my special associates. I spoke widely to my Leadership America colleagues, including Martha Farmer, executive director. I also called upon my League of Cities colleagues who had been council members and then mayors. Among them was Jessie Rattley of Newport News, Virginia, and Tom Bradley of Los Angeles. One of the Leadership America colleagues offered to move to Rochester to handle the campaign. Another friend offered to be my public relations person from her new position as a TV anchor in New York City. Each warned me that it was likely to be a dog fight, because I was breaking new ground by not only being a woman but by being black. They also predicted that there would be a crowd of candidates to fill a position that had been held by the same man for nearly two decades.

Many past supporters were rearing to go, but wanted an answer within a few days. Former campaign manager Kathy Sette was preoccupied with moving. Bill and I went through our usual facilitation with each other and decided to go for it. There were seven candidates and not enough press interest in someone who had stepped down from the limelight four years earlier. Some former supporters were determined to have a woman run and quickly moved on to support other candidates before I answered. Some volunteers joined my campaign in the hopes of defeating the run and still others played the dirty tricks within and outside of the campaign I had been warned about.

Some black preachers and liberal white women felt that a man should be the first African-American if there was to be one. With every campaign, some good things come about. Gaynell Wethers, multicultural department head at Nazareth College, formed a friendship with me over her voluntary campaign management. Bill and I vetoed our son and daughter coming home from college to spend full time in the campaign. Some of my ideas got copied by other campaigns, like my plan for the future of education in Rochester gleaned from a book co-written by me for the League of Cities on "Education Is Everybody's Business."

It is my hope that more women will seek the higher offices and that the news coverage will be more fair than in my campaign. One minister stopped me in the mall a few years ago to say, "Sister Scott, I just want to say I'm sorry. I was wrong in not supporting your run for mayor. You should have been mayor."

I was so astonished at the long-ago place from which I had moved on that it took a few moments to find the appropriate words for the obvious difficult admission. I looked at his wife, who had urged him to say those words. My thanks seemed an inadequate response, but it was the best I could muster at the moment. A few other well wishers still address me as Madam Mayor ... but it simply was not to be. Nor would I have wanted to give up the opportunities to help corporations and nonprofits address good community citizenship, diversity strategies and organizational effectiveness. I went on to attend the Tuck School of Business at Dartmouth and to work with Kay Iwatta, who shared with me her family history of surviving the camps where her family was interned by the U.S. government during World War II. I also worked with Roosevelt Thomas, renowned diversity strategist, on inclusion from Morehouse. My travels took me across the country and to meeting business women from Japan and Hawaii. Moving from being one of the few locally elected women in the mid 1970s to a successful business woman were the circles I had begun and handed to other women for the next generation. They will surely understand and find energy and possibility in the fact that a woman's place is truly in the House, the Senate, the presidency and heads of corporations—seats they can fill as well as any man.

One of the most effective public servants I have encountered in my travels is Assemblyman David Gant, dean of the Rochester delegation representing us in Albany. Among his opponents, he has the reputation for controlling and coercing the political scene, but I have found quite a different experience. David cares deeply about his constituents—all of them. At times, David would become angry about politicians who promised jobs and projects that would benefit his constituents if he would "organize his troops" to support them. When the benefits did not materialize, David became justifiably angry. Perhaps over the years a healthy mistrust of some Democratic Party bosses and politicians developed in this skilled Albany legislator.

He has always been very supportive of my service. From the beginning of our life in Rochester, Bill and I were invited to David's Rochester Black Leadership meetings, but because of Bill's music teaching schedule, I often attended alone. These meetings were brainstorming sessions intended to improve communications, share knowledge and empower our constituents to take control of their own lives. New laws, governmental announcements and special programs were often little understood, if they were known at all, among inner-city or unemployed people who may not read the newspaper or think that the news briefs on radio or television pertained to their lives. David took the issues and information to the people through the barber and beauty shops, community centers and churches. He also organized extensive voter-registration drives. His meetings were held all over Rochester—from the Nineteenth Ward to Baden Street Community Center to the community centers of FIGHT Square and Lena Gant Estates and neighborhood restaurants.

When I ran for president of city council, I knew that he informed long-time politicians that I had proven myself capable and was ready to be city council president. Some of his opponents, of course, later charged that his support of me for mayor of the city was in some way an extension of unlimited power for the "self-serving" David Gant. I do not recall a single instance when David attempted to dictate to me, unfairly influence me or coerce me away from my own conclusions.

David and I often shared the same views, and we share the commitment to encourage new voters and to teach people how to help themselves.

David's mother, Lena Gant, worked forty years to build neighborhood cohesion in the northeast section of the city. She helped found Jordan Community Health Center, the first neighborhood health center development in Rochester, and build Hanover Houses, the first low-income housing units funded by Housing and Urban Development (HUD).

Fifty years after the construction of the high-rise Hanover Houses, the run-down apartments were determined to be breeding grounds for crime and drug traffic. Chris Lindley and I, as council members, successfully lobbied the Department of Housing and Urban development, headed then by former National League of Cities President Henry Cisneros, and the city received HUD money to replace Hanover Houses with more livable townhouses and additional homes, which became known as Lena Gant Estates.

David dislikes recognition for himself, but it is my hope that someday an appropriate permanent recognition will be established of him and his mother's pioneering efforts in the poorer neighborhoods in our city.

Public Art in Our Community

As chair person of the National League of Cities Standing Committee on Community and Economic Development, I traveled to more than two dozen major cities in four years. We studied many strategies to revitalize and sustain quality city services and to broaden the base of citizen participation in the local community's economic success. I proposed a waterfront authority and development of the arts. I was impressed by how the housing issues were addressed, particularly by the Rausch Foundation. I could not get Mayor Tom Ryan to entertain the idea of Rausch's development in Rochester. Some cities early on developed their urban connection to the waterfronts. As long ago as the 19th century, noted landscape architect Frederick Law Olmsted identified Rochester's Genesee River and waterways as our central asset. But what most impressed me was public art. As art feeds the spirit, I believe it can be uplifting to everyone. Art was included in major economic and beautification efforts in Austin, Milwaukee, Seattle, Atlanta, Indianapolis, Los Angeles, Pittsburgh, Hartford and Baltimore.

While chairing one of the committee meetings in Phoenix, Arizona, I saw firsthand how public art as a universal language can move mountains of prejudgment and misunderstanding. While learning about the host community, we visited an Episcopalian church, whose white minister shepherded a congregation that was primarily white. The grounds were beautifully landscaped. The centerpiece of the grounds was a sculpture of the Birmingham black children who were killed in the Sunday School bombings in 1963. The artist sculpted them as these four- to six-year-olds would have looked had they been allowed to grow to full maturity. These three larger-than-life adult figures stood on a platform in the middle of a pond. Only one person at a time could walk on the path over the water and stand amidst the children whose arms were raised with hands clasping one another.

Such energy radiated from the sculpture that all seven members of the committee stood in stunned silence. It was the most moving work of public art I have ever experienced. I can still see the face of our African-American Atlanta, Georgia, council president, who began to weep uncontrollably. Our white host put her arm around her with an expression that asked, "What's wrong?"

She replied, "Nothing is wrong. But your placing this sculpture in Phoenix tells me that you care."

Witnessing what powerful artwork can do to remove distrust and fear made me determined to participate whenever possible in promoting art in our Rochester community.

I soon realized I was not the only Rochesterian promoting public art. I served on the committee to select artwork to be placed in the remodeled Rochester International Airport. It seems today tight budgets provide excuses to cut art projects. Somehow, the painting of cable boxes and placing of painted, molded fiberglass horses does not have the effect I was looking for.

Throughout my term on council, I encouraged money as a set-aside for public art in all city-controlled construction projects. I believe every community should have an art walk of some kind, because children surrounded by inspiring art objects and plantings become beautiful inside. My colleagues usually challenged these proposals with, "How much is that going to cost?" "Who's to say what art is?"

Betty Strasenburgh, Marian and Tom Hawks, and Kodak president Colby Chandler galvanized public support for the idea. Marian and Tom began to donate public art. Councilwoman Joan Hensler, Lois Geiss and I collaborated on efforts to regulate and eliminate visual pollution in inner cities by removing billboards. As Norma Brand, my first Rochester connection, lay dying of cancer she said to me, "The most important thing I have done in my life is to see to it that you and Joan Hensler became council members. Your plantings downtown and in neighborhoods, your creation of art and eliminating billboards in residential areas was a wonderful and inspirational improvement in Rochester's quality of life."

I introduced to city council and they approved the establishment of a blue-ribbon committee to study the importance of public art in Rochester, and a public art fund was established. Colby agreed to be honorary chair, but was so committed that he became one of the chief facilitators for what became known as the "Community Conversation on the Arts."

Citi Corp. Bank loaned an executive who performed so well that she was promoted to the New York City headquarters as worldwide community relations officer. She later took early retirement to become head of the New England Community Foundation. The committee found that there was overwhelming public support for the arts in Rochester and that a large part of the Rochester economy was driven by the arts, particularly evident in Kodak and the University of Rochester.

One of my proudest accomplishments was the support of the Writer in Residence position held by Ross Talerico. I facilitated the grant-supported position through the city's recreation department when Ross approached me on council and asked for my support. This program was a great outlet for students' expressions and an alternative to spending time in the streets. The writings that came out of this program might have given city leaders and teachers more insight into the escalating violence in the streets and in the schools.

Ross started the program for young people, but then expanded it to include nursing homes and senior citizens. He joined the youth and seniors to share their oral histories in prose and poetry. The city invited the participants to city hall for a reception. Surrounded by the fountains in the city hall atrium on the first floor, we listened as participants proudly read their work, and received applause and awards from council. I am saddened that the city did not continue this program.

Choices and Circles Enriching My Life

Two roads diverged in a wood, and I—I took the one less traveled by, and that has made all the difference. —Robert Frost

Though we think we know when we are young what we might do with our lives, we really do not know ourselves until we have the opportunities to make choices about what road we will walk down as we journey through life. I wanted a life of personal service and I had the skills to identify and solve problems, to find common ground among opposing parties and to bring people together, but I did not know how this dream would be fulfilled. Throughout my life, my work and volunteer service honed these skills and verified to me that I really was a woman suited to a life of family, public and community service. But, now that Bill and I have reached retirement age, I—for a fleeting moment—thought about the opportunities for personal wealth that we have turned down in preference for community service.

Early in our Rochester years, Bill and I had a financial planning meeting with an investment counselor. Coming from families with limited discretionary funds may have colored our reaction to at least one of the aggressive investment proposals this counselor made. He said that the money we give to charity could be turned into wealth if we invested it instead of giving it away. We knew how important individual community giving is to the welfare of its citizens. We couldn't imagine gaining personal wealth while others in our community went hungry or poorly clothed. It was clear to us that there was a values misfit between us and the financial planner.

My background and experience in the Nineteenth Ward Community Association and city council had given my credentials and personal values public exposure, attracting some tempting job offers from the private sector.

Three corporations—Kodak, Gannett and Xerox—offered me positions while I was on city council. The salaries would have made a significant difference in our family's lifestyle and disposable income. But taking these positions would have meant valuable time away from family. I have never regretted turning down the offers, though I do wonder where those roads would have led me. I would not have wanted to lose the shared experiences I have had with my family.

Looking back, Kodak offered me a position as a worldwide customer service representative. My job would have been to build networks between the company and neighborhoods, city government and congress. I had recently presented my research before the League of Cities, arguing for the importance of local governments providing tax-exempt bonding for local projects led by private companies. One Congressman remarked that my presentation before the Banking Committee was the most impressive and cogent he had ever heard. Perhaps this caught the attention of Kodak. I turned down this six-figure job offer because I did not want to give up my city council seat or travel extensively away from family.

The Gannett Foundation offered me a position that, indeed, captured my interest. Again, I would have had to give up the city council seat that I believe gave me the opportunity to make Rochester a better place to live.

I had managed the Charitable Trust for several years as the sole decision maker for a portion of the discretionary grants from Rochester Community Savings Bank, so I had the experience Gannett was looking for. I believe Gannett also offered me the position because of my work with the Ford Foundation in the early 1970s. Before being elected to council, I served on two think tanks for the Ford Foundation. One was on the improvement of the school principal's role in education, prompted by the then-recent Lighthouse Studies. I was also consultant to the Ford Foundation charged with determining whether a particular neighborhood had the contacts, infrastructure and credibility to be a strong engine of economic revitalization in such cities as Chicago, Detroit, Minneapolis, Seattle and Atlanta. As part of a team, I met with key players in the economic structures and neighborhood boards of the cities to determine if the neighborhoods that were potential recipients of grants had the ability to become successful. Some neighborhoods were approved and some were not.

One of the Ford Foundation's efforts in the 1960s and 70s was National Neighbors. They believed the CEO was having difficulty transitioning the organization from the local to the national level. Ford promised not to pull funding if one of the organization's goals would be to reach the national level by relocating the headquarters to Washington, D.C., and making a more comprehensive effort to cover the entire country. I found the work both interesting and challenging. For a few years, we were successful, but ACORN, a much more aggressive neighborhood organization, successfully challenged a Chicago bank on its right to pull out of inner-city neighborhoods. They were able to garner significant funding from local and national banks in collaborative projects with the poor neighborhoods and took a leading role in stopping the practice of red lining.

As president of National Neighbors, I worked hard to promote neighborhood racial integration. As I became more absorbed in my duties on city council, I was less engaged in the Nineteenth Ward Community Association activities or with their partner—National Neighbors. The secretary of Housing and Urban Development (HUD) under President Nixon appointed me as a HUD advisor because of my work in the neighborhoods.

A third corporate offer came from the Xerox Foundation. I would have been a nationwide sales representative, introducing salespeople to city government leaders who worked within the League of Cities. Xerox would have allowed me to stay on city council, but Bill and I were reluctant to let extensive travel diminish our family time.

The year I ran for mayor, another such opportunity came my way—to be a consultant for a school district and chamber of commerce in North Carolina to develop a strategy for raising the successful graduation rates of their rural and minority students. They literally begged me to consider the work, but my focus on being elected and my concern that I could not give them full attention caused me to turn down that job, which offered to pay me whatever I asked.

In addition to corporate offers, I was also approached by an intermediary of the federal government to check on my interest in being nominated as undersecretary of HUD. Relocating my family to Washington did not appeal to me. Finally, I was approached by the same party chair who had opposed my city council appointment to consider an appointment to the New York State Senate. Larry Kirwin, city and state Democratic party chair, tried to convince me that I was giving up an opportunity for significant wealth for our family's future, but because money had never been a driving force or a major value in my life over family and community service, the roads taken were simple choices for Bill and me.

We celebrated Christmas together at Rochester's City Hall.
Left to right: Gregory, June with daughter Shawneque, me, Crystal and Bill

Our Circle Grows

Bill and I, before we were even interested in each other, talked about what kind of family we wanted to have, the care of children and continuing the loving relationships between generations. Later, as our relationship became more serious, we discussed how many children we wanted. I naively said five or six. Bill swallowed hard and said we Scotts had fun with just two. We decided to make more decisions when the time came for such deliberations. Three was a good compromise. Besides, after having three children, my mother's comments came to mind: "You will know when your family is complete." Somehow, Crystal's birth gave me that feeling of completeness.

What should I share with posterity about our children? First and foremost, they are not perfect, but they are perfectly ours. My mother always said that about her own children. We encouraged them to be the best they could be without trying to change their basic natures.

Our children were "love made visible" as far as we were concerned, which is what I told my brother when he asked about Greg before he had a chance to see him. It was our hope before and after they were born to give them the discipline, experiences and the support necessary to enhance their lives without making them so busy they did not have time to be kids. Thus, we carefully chose the events to which they accompanied us. We welcomed neighborhood children to play with them and accompany us on trips to museums, appropriate church events, vacations, and school or neighborhood conventions and concerts. It would be most interesting to see what kinds of stories they would write about their own lives.

Our first child was Greg, born in Delevan, New York. In those days, it was considered special to give birth to a boy as your first born. We, of course, thought along with other members of our family, that he was beautiful. As the first grandchild in both families, his grandparents were especially proud. I overheard my dad saying of Greg on the only visit he made to see us during our married years, "You are one fine boy." All of our Delevan friends and Bill's colleagues took great pride in helping us raise him. Our friends, June and Wally Harrison (June later became Greg's kindergarten teacher), doted over him as a bright child.

We moved to Rochester when Greg was seven and June was three. Crystal was the only child born to us in Rochester. They enjoyed growing up together even if the girls did tease Greg so much about being adopted that he believed it for a period of time. Once Greg was so upset about the stringent rules of the household that he came downstairs with great stomping and blowing, mumbling that he was running away. Greg had always been so obedient that this came as a surprise to me and I was at a loss for words. He stood at the bottom of the steps for a while with tears streaming down his face. I asked, "What are you crying about?" He said, "Would you help me pack?" With an "a-ha" ringing in my mind, I said, "That's it. If you can't pack for yourself, you are too young to run away." And that was that.

One of Greg's gifts, which he probably gets from his father, is a wonderful, detailed memory. One day, the Rochester Police Department's Officer Friendly visited his elementary school. Greg came rushing into the house that day after school to use the phone (without asking permission). He was calling the police to tell them about what he thought was an abduction of a young child. He remembered the car in detail, color, style, license plate numbers, and the description of the man and woman in the car, as well as the child being forced to get into the car. Shortly after the

June and Greg celebrating the birth of Crystal and explaining to her that she better not suck her thumb because Grandpa Holland showed them how he lost fingers because he sucked them and accidentally bit them off. When the children and their cousins discussed Grandpa's stories later on, they discovered that he told each of them a different story depending upon the point he was trying to make.

Greg performing in *Ain't Misbehavin'* after college in the Downstairs Cabaret.

June performing in the Edison Tech Follies in her senior year.

policemen visited with Greg, they were able to find the child and discover that a parent had asked the grandparents to pick up the child because the parent had an emergency, but she had been told never to get into anyone's car without permission. The policemen amusedly said, "Are you sure you were not on the north side of town the other night about ten o'clock? We can't find anyone who remembers any details."

June was our second born in Delevan, New York. Greg, at four, had never seen an African-American baby at that point because we were the only African-American family in town. When we brought her home from the hospital wrapped in the blanket in the baby seat, Greg anxiously pulled the blanket away and said in delighted wonder and amazement, "She's brown just like me!" Bill was at the New York State Music Educator's conference in November when June was born. The doctor thought that Bill must have been flying low as he drove from the more than 450 miles away to get to the Buffalo hospital before supper.

I had thyroid surgery a few weeks after we brought June home from the hospital, so Grandma Scott came to care for her. When I was finally able to hold June, she would only stay in my arms for a little while and then would cry to go back to her crib or play pen. That independence continued throughout her growing-up years. The first incident that confirmed her development in the direction of independence was when she was nearly four. As with all children, she did not like to have her hand held when crossing the street. She looked up at me one day and said, "Don't you want me to grow up?"

"Of course I do," I said.

Her reply was, "Then why won't you let me cross the street by myself?"

When June took flute lessons, her teacher said she had the most natural "embouchure." (How you place your lips on the instrument.) However, June was loath to practice. She gave up the lessons, but played the flute for her first baby. June's art teachers were interested in having her pursue art as a career, but that has been on hold for several years. However, I have had two of her paintings framed to hang in our kitchen.

Crystal was born in our third year in Rochester after a wonderful day at the Nineteenth Ward Square Fair. She, too, was beautiful and independent from the day of her birth.

All of the children are creative in different ways. Bill and I took them

Crystal performing in *Dead Dog Gulch*. She won the lead role by memorizing the lines of every role.

Crystal in the city hall atrium reading her oral history and poetry.

to stage plays in New York City, musicals and movies, and watched reasonable family-friendly television shows. They all love the theater. For their sixteenth birthdays, each one was allowed to choose a trip, including a stage play. June chose *Dream Girls* in New York City and Crystal chose *Nunsense* in Toronto. We exposed them to dance and instrumental lessons. The Rochester City School District had a wonderful music education and performance program, as did Hochstein Music School's Orff (an introduction for toddlers to music) Program and children's choir. Twice over the Christmas season, Crystal was able to participate in the children's small ensemble, performing Haydn's *Toy Symphony* with the Rochester Philharmonic. As a student, daughter June participated as a singer and dancer in every one of the Edison Tech High School Follies.

Greg's creativity led him to be engaged in the theater during high school, college and in his early adult life. He was so engaged in nighttime stage building at Syracuse University that he often missed an early-morning English class until we found out. When he moved to Alfred University, although he was an engineering major, many of his best friends came out of the theater department, where he could often be found being of assistance as a prompter and stage hand. As a young adult, he played lead roles in such plays as *Godspell* and *Ain't Misbehavin'* at the Downtown Cabaret in Rochester. Greg also sings classical and Christian church music. He, his wife, Shevonne, and family also participate in church theater.

Crystal is our "Jill of all creative things." She started writing poems, as many children do, at an early age and soon discovered that she was especially gifted with putting words together in unusual ways. She was as gifted as any of the students I taught in English. She participated in school plays from an early age. When in second or third grade, she memorized the whole play before tryouts in order to secure a role. Ross Talerico, who started a program with the Rochester Recreation Department, indicated that Crystal was an excellent poet and writer of oral histories.

Whenever the children participated in school plays, concerts or church programs, it was by their choice and not our orchestration. One of us was always present for performances. We did insist that each one of them take piano lessons. What else would be the case when your father is a vocal director and pianist and your mother could hardly pass a piano in her youth without touching the keys to see how they sounded. Each child decided after four or five books (grades) of lessons that they

Grandson Barry modeling for Princess Conte, designer of African wear for children.

Greg, Shevonne, her commanding officer and children Malcom, Sekayi and Sienna when they were chosen as the Air Force family of the year on Sheppard Air Force Base in Texas.

would promise to continue to play for fun if they could simply leave off the lessons and practice. I suspect they coached each other on this compromise of practice and performance. Each also took lessons with the world-renowned Garth Fagan Dance. Garth is the celebrated dance master and award-winning choreographer of *The Lion King*. The kids speak fondly of those times. Greg also studied trombone.

Although we did not allow the children to play one against the other, there were times when one of us was more sympathetic to a child's distress than the other. Bill often was strict with behavior issues, but quick to sense when one of ours needed his sympathy. In my busyness, I sometimes moved too fast to always take time to be sensitive. But we took turns without actually discussing it. We believe that children should always have some place to turn when feeling neglected or unduly disciplined. Thus, we also made friends with other families who had children the ages of ours and whose ideals and lifestyles would reinforce our beliefs. Many of those families lived on our street on Arvine Heights in the Nineteenth Ward of Rochester. The Kamells, our friends and neighbors across the street, and the Lesures, two doors down, were good advisors and confidantes for our children. They are both lifelong friends. The neighborhood also supported the annual selling of cookies and other goodies for scouts, church, and performance groups and schools our children attended.

Early in our marriage, we and our parents decided not to insist on holiday visits. We have also encouraged our adult children to create their own unique holiday traditions separate from ours. Summertime provided extended times with our parents. Also, having the children spend several weeks with them alone was our way of cementing the bonding between generations. Greg, June and Crystal attended the Albion College Adventure in the summers after they reached the eleven-year-old threshold. Since Albion remained my parents' home, that gave Dad and Mom additional contact with their grandchildren. Greg even spent a summer working as a playground attendant for the Albion Recreation Department. It helped that one of my classmates and Dad's mentee, Tilman Cornelius, was the head of the recreation department.

We are proud that our children have grown up to be independent followers of their own dreams. Greg is the human resource director of Doctors and Clinics of West Texas. He and his very talented wife, Major Shevonne Scott, have three children, Sekayi, eleven, born in Japan; Malcolm, nine; and Sienna, six, going on ninety-nine. Their family

One of my duties on Rochester City Council was to welcome VIPs. Daughter Crystal was not too happy on realizing that this Mickey Mouse whose face showed under the mask was not the "real" Mickey Mouse that she saw at Disney World.

carries on in the traditions of both their parents in reaching out to others and especially to youth. Shevonne and Greg have chaired youth and adult ministries in the various churches where Shevonne has been stationed. They were designated as the "base family of the year" by the Sheppard Air Force Base in 2008.

Our daughter June and her husband, Barrett, have four children: Shawnequa Lockett, 23, who is studying to become a nurse; Barrett Jr., enrolled in criminal justice at Finger Lakes Community College; Barry, a high school junior; and Bryant, a fifth-grader.

Crystal received her BA from the University of Iowa and plans to pursue an MFA in film writing in the near future. She is an avid Iowa fan. She, too, has continued to write and has developed a strong portfolio. She worked at Geva, Rochester's live theater, as a stage hand and was an extra in *To Kill a Mockingbird*. She has taken good care of us as, Bill had a knee replacement and I am recovering from a silly accident with a city garbage truck hitting a car behind which I was standing. Crystal is also my computer buff.

During my elected-office days, Crystal, as the youngest, often accompanied me on parade rides, special events and meetings with officials. She was just five when I was first elected to serve on council. June was in her late teens and young people would rather not be seen with their parents. Greg was already off to college when Crystal officiated with me.

Each of the children, our granddaughter and Bill at one time or another has worked in my company, Scott Associates, as materials specialists, researchers, facilitators, secretaries, bookkeepers and assistants. It is they who have allowed me to be a reasonable steady mom and businesswoman. Our business, Scott Associates, was cited by *Working Woman's Magazine* as one of five top organizations in the country.

When we ask our children what they enjoyed most about their growing-up years, one of the things they mention is that they felt enriched by our attempts to keep them connected to a very busy and dispersed extended family—a cadre of aunts, uncles and cousins throughout the United States, as well as my special childhood friends.

We visited often with my brothers and their families. June's son came to live with us several summers and journeyed with us to Riverside, California, when brother Bill was a professor of history at the University of California. We and my siblings' families on the Holland side spent several summer holidays at Martha's Vineyard in Massachusetts and at Elmhurst in Canada at a small campsite. In Canada, we chose cabins over tents. The children learned to fish at Elmhurst and to collect shells and stones at Martha's Vineyard. Cousin Jerry Holland's daughter Kim from Detroit spent a summer vacation with us. Niece Pamela and her mother Ophelia visited us.

We have started to give our grandchildren some of those travel experiences by taking the Johnsons and Shawnequa to Canada's Science

Bill's brother Percy and his niece Pamela shared Christmas with us for a number of years at 30 Arvine Heights. Being the only two children in his family made them close as adults. It was good for my children to get to know their Uncle Percy and cousin Pam.

Bill and Percy

Brother Bob and his wife Barb seated in front with their granddaughter. Standing left to right: Jackie holding Kheri and Tolbert Tillman's son Tolbert; Bob's son Robb; Tolbert Tillman and his wife Kheri holding their daughter

Claudia and brother Bill Holland and their sons, Todd and Jamie.

Our friend John Wilson was instrumental in helping nephew David get enrolled to finish his senior year in Rochester. Sister June was proud to attend her son's graduation.

Family reunion in Cleveland, Ohio, organized by sister June. Hollands from Detroit and friends from everywhere gathered together. Left to right: brother Bill, Mayor of Albion; Charles (Bucky) and wife, Diane Jones. Second row: Me, cousin Robert Holland, sister June, Vernell Sims, cousin Jerry Holland, Hosey Hall, Bob's wife Barbara Holland. Third row: Bill Scott, Brother Bob, Brother Bill's wife Claudia, Benny Sims. My dad urged Bucky to run for mayor of Albion because he did not have the stamina himself after lung surgery. He believed Bucky to be well-suited for the position.

Bob, me and Bill at Bill and Claudia's Pennsylvania home. Bill was Chief Human Resources Officer for the University of Pennsylvania. We were there to enjoy the Penn races—a special event where outdoor track teams still compete. Many teams went on to the Olympics.

June's children, Crystal and me celebrating Easter Sunday. Left to right: Grandchildren Barry, Do, June holding Bryant. Second row: Me, granddaughter Shawnequa and daughter Crystal.

Photo by Denise Batiste Photography.

Our great-grandson Jerimiah recognizing himself in the mirror as his father, Barrett Jr., holds him up.

Photo by Denise Batiste Photography.

Renee Gantt drove with her father to our 50th wedding anniversary celebration, where she discovered her photograph as a flower girl in our wedding. Her father, my cousin Herbert, had always told her there were no wedding photographs of her because she would not keep still.

Museum, to Washington, D.C., and to Disneyland in California.

We still get complaints from our children that we did not take them to the Bahamas, Japan, France, England or Hawaii, where we have visited three times. We thought, in the tradition of their independent natures, they could make those trips for themselves. Bill and I enjoyed our time alone together. Crystal made good on that idea by taking exciting voyages to China and Puerto Rico.

Our Christmas holiday tradition, which has been the most consistent special celebration with the whole Bill and Ruth Scott family, is to invite the family that is able to be present to brunch. We have a Christmas tree that most likely Crystal and her dad have decorated on Christmas Eve under which all of the family gifts are placed and not opened until after brunch on the 25th. It is my job to decorate the living room with various ornaments, some of which we have had since the early days of our marriage. Before brunch, we ask each person seated around the table to tell a part of the Christian Christmas story or tell for what they are most thankful. We then share a table spread with such foods as homemade coffee cakes, breads, omelets reminiscent of Bill's youth, cheese and non-cheese grits, sausage, ambrosia, a recipe from my growing-up days of pineapple, orange slices and coconut and orange juice, milk, coffee and tea.

After brunch, we open presents by calling out the names from under the tree. Bill loves the wrapping of gifts and is often up Christmas Eve long after others have gone to bed, doing his annual wrapping. He has heard the Christmas message from the Vatican. We believe in the church universal and that singing and this message are a part of our tradition. There are always a few gifts from Santa to Mrs. Santa and vice versa. There is also always a small gift wrapped many times over until it looks like a large gift. The excitement always grows as the children wonder to which person Grandpa Scott made the trick gift for this year.

Not the Final Chapter!

As we celebrated our 50th wedding anniversary by renewing our wedding vows, we reflected back on our lives—on a more personal level than we had already for this memoir. We have had the blessing of living long lives in relatively good health. We have been blessed with wonderful community-spirited children.

Bill was recalling that some of his former students stop him to tell him how much he has influenced their lives as a music teacher. Bill did teach music—but along with it he taught the spirit, power and wisdom that this universal language speaks. His students traveled through many walks of life, but always with that glad step that music taught them. Bill is still teaching and serving as Voice Department chairman, now at Hochstein School of Music, named for a promising young violinist whose life was cut short just days before the Armistice was signed in 1918. His students now carry that promise through the 21st century.

In much the same way, I also continue to work, as I will until I draw my last breath—maybe even a number of years after. History unfolds too slowly for me sometimes. But in my life, I have seen a lot of change—women have come to be more than 50% of the voting population, they have been elected to important political positions, one has been a major party presidential candidate, and more and more young women of all colors, and nationalities now seek leadership positions outside of the home and boxes that once confined us in history.

Just as other women have greatly influenced my life, I hope my own and the sharing of my journey to discover who I am and who I was meant to be has a lasting influence on others.

As the times change, I find myself evaluating the world and our role in it. Periodically, I attend and often speak before groups of young, aspiring, diverse community leaders whose energy I want to harness and help them find the right direction with the power of their own circles.

I have a different reflection every day that reminds me of the "long way" we have come as women and African-Americans. I now recall a beautiful day I stood on the veranda of 1600 Pennsylvania Avenue waiting to be called in to an advisory session with President Carter. We were asked to share our insights and expertise on Urban Policy. I was then Rochester city council member.

Of all the roads we choose to take throughout our lives, I was pleasantly surprised to meet up with my old childhood friend Beverly Thompson. She was a political leader in Dallas, Texas, here in Washington for the same Urban Policy advisory session I was to attend. We laughed and reminisced together as we had when we were little girls. I felt like one of my circles in life had been completed.

The passing of seasons refreshes our spirits and bids us to celebrate our expanding circles in family, neighborhood, church and friendships. We still engage in a community that continues to reshape itself at the edge of old and new social changes and economic realities.

As for me, I shall continue to *"look up and laugh and love and lift."* (From *I Would Be True,* a youth missionary hymn.)

Photo by Denise Batiste Photography.

College classmate Dorothy Lennox helping me dress for my renewal-of-vows ceremony for our 50th wedding anniversary.

Photo by Denise Batiste Photography.

Bill and I danced at our 50th wedding anniversary celebration in 2011. A minister at our wedding a half a century before wished for us to go through life making beautiful music together—and we still are.

How Can Black Bards Sing?
–Ruth Holland Scott

We had cornered the
Market of lost dreams
And stars that seemed out of reach.
The mortuary tables of ambitions
Thwarted our expectations,
But all the while we slaved.
Nobody knew about our spirits that grew
from the ashes of our discontent,
crossed Jordan so many times
we weren't afraid to die.
The question asked about Black Bards singing
'Tis an inappropriate one …
'Cause we have always sung.

Who Are We?
–Ruth Holland Scott

In life
are we physical beings having
a spiritual experience—or
are we spiritual beings having
a physical experience?

The creator of circles knows.